INSIDE
THE WORLD
OF
BIG-TIME
MARATHONING

The International Running Center, home of the New York Road Runners Club, located at 9 East 89 Street, New York, NY 10128; (212) 860-4455 *(Courtesy Sofia Shafquat)*

INSIDE THE WORLD OF BIG-TIME MARATHONING

Fred Lebow
With Richard Woodley

Rawson Associates • New York

The New York City Marathon is the culmination of the efforts of hundreds of individuals and groups that pull together to make their common vision into reality. My heartfelt admiration and thanks go to more people than I could possibly name here. I would like to dedicate this book to all the volunteers, organizations and city agencies whose unfailing energy and dedication make the Marathon possible, to the sponsors who have believed in us every step of the way, and to the more than 23,000 loyal members of the New York Road Runners Club and Club's Board of Directors.

FRED LEBOW

Library of Congress Cataloging in Publication data

Lebow, Fred.
  Inside the world of big-time marathoning.
  Includes index.
  1. New York City Marathon, New York, N.Y.—History.
2. Lebow, Fred. 3. Sports promoters—United States—
Biography. I. Woodley, Richard. II. Title.
GV1065.22.N49L43   1984   338.4'77964'26   83-43110
ISBN 0-89256-262-5

Published simultaneously in Canada by McClelland and Stewart Ltd.
Packaged by Sandra Choron, March Tenth, Inc.
Composition by Folio Graphics Co., Inc.
Manufactured by Fairfield Graphics, Fairfield, Pennsylvania
Designed by Stanley S. Drate
First Edition

It was as dramatic a scene as ever could have been fashioned by the gods of old Greece: in the rain, the winning runner on his knees, his arms raised thankfully to the sky; behind him, the valiant loser, crumpled on his back, his eyes closed in exhaustion, pain, defeat. Rod Dixon, of New Zealand, had won the New York City Marathon, catching England's Geoff Smith after twenty-six miles, passing him within sight of the finish banner, to win by a few seconds.

I might have seemed like an alien intruder on this heroic moment, a lean bearded man in a bicycle cap running around like a frantic parent, waving my arms to bring medical attention to Smith, then running over to embrace Dixon. I *did* feel parental. I was flooded with excitement and relief and gratitude and pride. I had been a founder of this marathon thirteen years before. I was director of it now. I was president of the club that produced it. I was the visible top of a less visible pyramid of workers, supporters, civic officials, and road-racing experts who together had created the setting for one of the most dramatic finishes in the history of our sport.

I was old enough to be the father of these men who had dueled to the limits of their physical and mental abilities to provide the incredible drama witnessed by millions. And like a parent, I was overcome with the pride and gratitude that come to one who has seen his boys perform beyond the public's expectations and validate the old man's claims and faith.

Minutes from now, Grete Waitz, of Norway, would cross the line to win the women's race. My fulfillment would be complete.

Although the old Greeks, who originated the marathon run, might have blessed the international heroics, they couldn't have matched the quality of competition or the breadth of the audience. Two and a half million spectators witnessed the 26.2-mile race through the five boroughs of New York City; 30 million more watched on worldwide television. The winners ran at speeds equaled or surpassed by no more than a handful of runners ever in the world. As important for me was the fact that more than fifteen thousand people from sixty-eight countries completed our race—testimony both to the appeal of marathoning in the world today and to the quality of organization, preparation, and allure of the New York City Marathon.

In the rush of celebrative events immediately following the winning of the marathon—the cheers and congratulations, the attentions to the recovery of totally spent athletes, the crowning of the winners with laurel wreaths, the presentation of the winners to the international press—it occurred to me that a private milestone of historic proportions had been passed.

As of the completion of the 1983 New York City Marathon, with all the top, world-class runners now across the line, the total amount of prize money we had paid over the years to the highest finishers in New York had reached $1 million.

One million dollars! It was a measure of both what the marathon had been and what it had become. For most of those years the payments to elite "amateur" runners in our marathon had been secret, "under the table," because the international amateur rules forbade them. Now the rules had changed, the payments were legitimately made, properly sanctioned by the organizations governing the sport. That the prize money was still, in 1983, a hidden matter in New York was only because of reluctance of the city government to make it known. But that was bound to be only a temporary accommodation—a grace period during which the city could accustom itself to the new realities of international marathoning.

The growth of prize money, from illegal to legal, from small amounts to large ones, was the symbol of the evolution of the marathon in just a few years—in what seemed, to me, overnight.

I thought back to that sunny, 80-degree morning of September 13, 1970, when we held the first New York City Marathon. Four laps around Central Park. We had 126 official starters and just 55 finishers—and even fewer spectators. It was nothing more than an unpublicized curiosity to those few who saw it or heard about it. Outside of the Boston Marathon and the Olympics, hardly anybody knew anything about marathons. Visitors to the park that first day didn't even know what was going on. They gawked or smiled or even laughed at the small parade of men struggling by in short pants. We spent less than one thousand dollars on the whole event, most of it out of my own pocket to buy sodas for everybody and cheap wristwatches for the top finishers.

If hardly anybody knew anything about marathons, nobody knew me. There was no reason to. I was just a bearded forty-year-old immigrant from Rumania who spoke with a strange accent and worked in the Garment District. I ran in that race. I finished forty-fifth, so I didn't even get one of my own wrist-watches.

Now, in 1983, we had 17,000 entrants—and turned away 44,000 more. The whole city turned out, and a large segment of the country and even a piece of the rest of the world tuned in to us on TV. Our budget for this one marathon was $1.3 million, and the top finishers pulled in a total of about $200,000 in prize money.

And I, the marathon director, was treated like a big cheese. I don't get to run our marathon anymore because I am too busy directing it from a lead car surrounded by walkie-talkie operators. But people give me wristwatches all the time. And clothes and meals and trips, all manner of tributes to this unanticipated status.

It is mind-boggling to me, when I stop to look at it, how in a little more than a decade everything in road racing is a thousand times bigger—number of races around the world from a couple of miles to marathons; number of runners; size of budgets. No other sport in history has had such an incredible spurt of growth in such a short time. Now there are seven hundred marathons throughout the world, three hundred in the United States. This country alone has over 30 million recreational runners, 2 million of whom have run a marathon someplace. Ten years ago the mile run, on a track, was track and field's glamour event. Now it's the marathon.

A decade ago, when I became its president, the New York Road Runners Club had a couple hundred members and a budget of a couple hundred dollars. Now, with 24,000 members, we are the largest running club in the world—perhaps the largest athletic club of any kind. We own our own building and have fifteen computer terminals in our offices. I no longer work in the Garment District. I am full-time president of the club. We have an annual nonprofit operating budget of $4 million. We have a paid staff of thirty-five. Senior staff members and I get invited around the world to consult on marathons and run in them. We helped organize, or were the model for, many of the world's marathons—London, Berlin, Helsinki, Seoul, Tel Aviv, Montreal, Honolulu, and others. Four years ago we founded the Association of International Marathons (AIMS), which now consists of forty-one of the major marathons of the world. Its purpose is to promote international marathoning, develop more uniform standards, and influence the policies governing the sport at the highest levels.

The New York City Marathon has become the centerpiece in the expansion of international marathoning because of the extraordinary support of the city—the government and the financial community and the public. Before the recent Olympics, Peter V. Ueberroth, president of the Los Angeles Olympic Organizing Committee, said: "I think the best sporting event in this country is the New York City Marathon, because people embrace that event."

That embrace has provided us with the tools for development of a superb organization for production of such a high-quality event. Bill Rodgers won our race four straight times, and his name became a household word. Alberto Salazar won it three times and set the world record. Grete Waitz won five times and three of those times set women's world records. Allison Roe, from New Zealand, set yet another world record for women. We've even appeared in the *Guinness Book of Records* for having the all-time greatest number of spectators for any sporting event— 2.5 million, an attendance we've maintained for four years.

And now we had a new men's champion, Rod Dixon, the 1983 winner. The crowd had seen another great race between two brand-new stars. And despite being drenched by the chilly rain, nobody was leaving. They waited for Grete Waitz to appear in her fifth women's triumph. And they waited after that to cheer the more than fifteen thousand runners that would follow the winners, straining, pounding, spending their last energy to finish the race just as the winners had.

With the crowd yelling, the television cameras whirring, masses of press photographers snapping away, and the main field of ordinary runners now flooding across the finish line, it was a huge, beautiful, loud storm of celebration and success that enveloped me. At such a moment you feel as if you are at the center of the world.

At the end of every one of our marathons I think: How can we top this one? How can the euphoria of any future marathon match what we are all feeling now? Sometimes I even get pretty down for a couple of days afterward, feeling lonely, empty, like maybe the best part of my life has passed. Yet every year there are new excitements. Every year it all works better. Every year it gets bigger. Every year it is more complicated, more challenging, more successful, more rewarding.

Every year there is more money involved. It is, in its way, big business now, and sometimes that distracts attention from the more important aspects. More important than money is the fact that the marathon is a big, happy event, the biggest event of the year in New York City, and it welds the entire town together. Most of the national and international attention is focused on the elite runners, the winners. But to those of us who put the race together, what is best of all is not just the stars, but the thousands of ordinary runners who surmount their own private struggles to complete the 26.2-mile distance and become part of the celebration.

This is in no way a how-to-run-a-marathon book. If I am expert about anything, it is not about *how* to run. I am one of those ordinary, middle-of-the-pack runners for whom winning is just completing the race. What I can't do in quality I try to make up for in quantity. I run too much. In the fifteen years since I started running I have run fifty-seven marathons. In the last thirty-one months I have run thirty-one. Trying to fulfill this odd midlife quota of running one marathon a month has produced, especially in the past year, a number of running disasters. But my travels allow me to run marathons all over the world, and since I have a craving to complete as many marathons as possible in as many different places as possible, that's what I do.

I sometimes wonder why I run so much, and at least a partial answer may be this: Directing the New York City Marathon is the biggest thing in my life. It is a matter of deepest satisfaction to help put it together, and it is exciting to be in the lead car ahead of the runners. But it is also terribly frustrating not to be running in our own marathon. By running in other places the rest of the time, and especially by running another marathon just before ours, I am at least guaranteed a set of perpetually tired legs to ease some of the frustration.

Meanwhile, the New York City Marathon continues to grow and prosper. And that's where the money comes in.

If you want to produce a big and well-organized marathon for the mass and for the elite, which accommodates the most runners possible in the most fun and exciting and safe and satisfying way, you have to have money. A proper course well supervised, big crowds and efficient crowd control, medical, security, and support services of all kinds, accurate computer timing and scoring, various hospitalities, parties, handouts, and hoopla—the whole wide range of thousands of large and small details that allow us to give personal attention to every single runner—that costs a lot of money.

You attract money by putting on a great show and attracting attention. You attract attention by attracting big names. That is the reality.

Since we want to put on a great show, for years we have, from time to time, been paying some elite, world-class runners under the table as part of their inducement to race in New York. The payments had to be under the table to protect their amateur status—primarily for Olympic eligibility. It was a common practice with major marathons. Now it can be done legitimately, and virtually every marathon does it. Because a road race of 26.2 miles is so grueling and depleting, the top competitive runners—those good enough to win or finish in the top ten or twenty—can "peak" or prepare adequately for only two or three serious marathons a year. With seven hundred marathons around the world bidding for the best runners, competition to attract them is fierce.

What we pay some of the elite athletes is only part of their inducement to race in New York. Some other marathons now pay more. But since New York is the media capital of the world, a New York winner can get rich through appearances and commercial endorsements if he or she knows how to capitalize on winning. Beyond the money the elite runners, like all the rest, want to be part of a good, well-directed, well-attended show. And that's what we concentrate on giving them here. Payments to athletes are only a small part of a budget.

The New York Road Runners Club puts on more than one hundred races a year, at distances ranging from the one-mile 5th Avenue Mile to the 6-Day Run of more than five hundred miles, races for everyone from beginners to the highest ranking in the world. For these we have our paid staff, helped by several hundred volunteers. At the club we also have $300,000 worth of computers in whose memory banks for instant retrieval are included not only vital statistics of age, address, and running records of every top road racer in the world but also those of every entrant in each one of our races.

At marathon time we hire more people, and on marathon day there are 4,500 volunteers (more than one for every four runners) working virtually around the clock at the club and on the course from long before the start to long after the finish. In addition, for the marathon we incorporate another $200,000 worth of donated computer equipment, which allows instant tabulation of time, place, age, etc., of every finisher and almost instant publication of results. (In 1983 postcards notifying every finisher of his or her personal time and placement were mailed marathon night.) It is the fastest, most sophisticated, most complete marathon computer system in the world.

Add to our 1983 marathon budget of $1.3 million another half million dollars' worth of city services—police, parks, highways, sanitation, and more—and you get a part of the picture.

Further, what makes a marathon such as ours especially attractive are the resources poured into the event to focus world attention on it. Three elements have to come together at once: top runners, big sponsors, and network television. In negotiating for all that, you orchestrate a kind of self-fulfilling promise: Convince the runners that there will be big sponsors and network television; convince sponsors that there will be network television and top runners; convince television that there will be top runners and big sponsors. If everybody believes in it, it all happens as promised—provided you deliver a topflight event as a consequence.

But the key is that *all* the runners benefit from this organization and money, not just the elite. Our strength is still the grass roots—the ordinary runners and the volunteers who support them. However big we are or become, our foundation and primary concern will be the grass roots. It is the increase in numbers of ordinary runners—not the elite—that causes our marathon to grow each year. Almost 100,000 people have run the New York City Marathon in its fourteen years. If we could accept everybody who wants to run our marathon, we might have 100,000 *per year*. We limit the field only to what we can accommodate with safe controls and support services.

Of course, when you get into something of this size and

complexity, not everything is smooth and neat and clean. With all the money involved there is a lot of behind-the-scenes wheeling and dealing, politics, power plays, bargaining, cajoling, arm twisting, ego soothing, mutual back scratching—all sorts of the maneuvering that goes into any ambitious growth industry. Here are some of the complexities we will explore in later pages:

We have to deal with governments, from that of New York City, for the services we need, to the governments of Iron Curtain countries, to get the runners we want.

We have to deal with the International Amateur Athletic Federation (IAAF), which is the world governing body for amateur athletics; with The Athletics Congress (TAC), which is the U.S. governing body for track and field; and with all manner of other organizations and special-interest groups lobbying for their own causes.

We deal with the directors of other marathons in the United States and around the world, sometimes to help each other out, sometimes to argue over who's getting what share of the wealth of runners, publicity, or power.

We deal with runners, in this context meaning the elite, invited ones. It used to be simpler. We'd just call them up and say, "Come and run New York." Price was relatively modest and easy to work out. Now marathon runners have become superstars. They have agents. An agent's job is to get more money. Sometimes they try to play us off against other marathons.

We deal with sponsors. It used to be a hassle just to *get* sponsors. Now we get more offers than we can accept. It matters to us what potential sponsors represent and whether their companies have class. We even have a "Good Taste Committee" to oversee such things. There is still a lot of loyalty between us and our original sponsors. But of course every year we need more money, they want more exposure in return, new sponsors want to come in, there are more big events to sponsor, and there's a lot of horse trading.

We deal with the press. In general, the press has been very good to us. I am usually open with them. Sometimes maybe too open. It ruffles official feathers, especially in the business world, where they are used to a more cozy style. Some people think we get too much press, and some people think I am a *creation* of the press. Publicity and promotion are, to be sure, primary concerns of mine. We negotiated a modest contract with network television four years ago, when we were a much smaller commodity. Now we are about to negotiate a new contract. We are worth a lot more. So it will not be so simple. Now we have leverage to get other events covered, beyond the marathon.

Internally, too, there are negotiations. The club has a board of directors. Some of them have been around longer than I have. Not everybody on the board likes the way I do things. Not everybody on the staff does, either. Nor do all the members of the club. A couple of years ago there was a move to unseat me. Some people in our own organization think I am drunk with power, high-handed. That perception is also held by some within the IAAF, TAC, the city administration, and other marathons.

A simple answer could be that I don't care. I do, actually, but not enough to spend a lot of time trying to please everybody. The New York Road Runners Club and the New York City Marathon have become what they are because of the efforts of myself and a lot of other people who cooperate in the dream to make what we do the best that is done anywhere, and for the most people. Small thinkers, doubters, whiners can drag you down. I ignore them when I can. I ignore small problems, petty squabbles, nit-picking protests. Some people think I ignore important problems and even important people. I have been called a tsar, a tyrant, an egomaniac, a male chauvinist, a cynical politician, a shameless power broker, a dictator, an emperor, a despot (even an enlightened despot).

Believe it or not, you can hear or read all these things about yourself and not be disturbed. Because virtually every weekend of every year, our club is putting on a race of some kind for hundreds or even thousands of runners. And because there's that one Sunday in every October when it all culminates in the New York City Marathon.

Naturally, there are people who wish all this expansion had

never happened. They yearn for those earlier days when marathon running was an obscure sport for just a few men (and no women), and there wasn't any hoopla about it. But that is just the point: The sport didn't reach anybody.

In New York there was a small clique of men who got together on weekends to run in the Bronx. It was like a secret society or a poker game among the boys. In 1969 I had just started running on my own, by myself, and I was looking for races of some kind. I discovered this group, joined it (treated like an outsider at first), quickly came to relish the races, and thought the whole thing should be expanded. By the time I became president of the New York Road Runners Club in 1972, the first and main thing I wanted to do was promote running. I got involved because I ran. I wanted everybody to run. I wanted women to run—a radical idea then.

In 1976, at about the time we moved the New York City Marathon out of the confines of Central Park and routed the course through all five boroughs of the city (a major elevation in status and all kinds of logistical and safety risks), the running boom hit.

Suddenly, everybody was running and talking about running. Physical fitness was the rage, and running was the best way to achieve it. Our marathon was on the crest of the wave. Jim Fixx's *The Complete Book of Running,* destined to become a longtime number-one best seller, was brought out to coincide with the date of our 1977 marathon. The running boom had turned into an all-out explosion. Running was good for everybody and everything. It made you a better person. It improved your sex life. (Runners may or may not be better lovers, but I'll tell you this: More romances are launched on the running course than in singles bars.) Running fixed everything.

Running became the subject of so many articles, so much conversation, so much attention all over the place, that it created a backlash. Backlashers saw it as just another extravagant fad, like hula hoops, or worse: It was even dangerous—to your knees, your organs, your marriage, whatever.

Of course, it was not a fad. Running didn't fix everything, but the real benefits were clear and enduring: You *did* feel better, your body *did* perform better, you *did* enjoy the camaraderie of other runners, who were fit and energetic people. And you could eat all you wanted and not get fat.

And so the sport grew as no other sport has. It will continue to grow because it is still largely a middle-class or upper-middle-class sport, and there are still large segments of the population we have yet to reach.

The basic premise of the running boom is that it is good for and accessible to people of all ages, all incomes, both sexes. You don't even have to be an athlete. At minimal cost you put on a pair of running shoes, a pair of shorts, a T-shirt; anyone can run a little. Gain a little fitness, you can run a couple of miles, then maybe a 10-kilometer race, eventually maybe even a marathon. Almost anyone—given patience, time for training, persistence—can run a marathon. And completing a marathon run, for people who aren't necessarily young or otherwise athletic, is a particularly heroic physical accomplishment at a stage or state in life when few if any opportunities for heroic physical accomplishment are within reach. Anyone who has done it will tell you: Few things in their lives match the thrill of finishing their first marathon.

Regardless of all the ritual that has developed around the sport, the basic premise still applies. The simplicity of running is the heart and soul of the sport. The ordinary, everyday runners are the mainstream. I can never forget this because I am one of them, regardless of what else I am.

2

Before getting into the intricacies, conflicts, and excitements of the years from the beginning, I'd like to show recent evolution through the story of my relationship with one runner, Bill Rodgers.

Nobody epitomizes the evolution of the sport and its paradoxes better than Rodgers. Rodgers, from Boston, won the New York City Marathon four straight times—1976–79—and because of his success and his open, innocent, engaging personality, he captured the hearts of everyone interested in running as nobody else has.

I haven't had a crazier relationship with any other runner. Personally, in private, Billy is impossible not to like. He is honest, delightfully outspoken without a hint of meanness; he has a flaky, Peter Pan–like quality. Through all the years we've known each other we've maintained steady friendship, gone out to dinner together, had fun times.

At the same time, publicly, nobody has given me a worse press, tried to discredit me more, occasionally irked me more, than he has. It is a paradox I cannot fathom, and so simply accept.

Billy has long been one of the more outspoken runners among those against the hypocrisy of under-the-table payments, arguing that runners should be entitled to the dignity of forthright prize money like athletes in other fields. In principle I have always agreed with him.

Yet Billy was the first runner I agreed to pay—under the table. That was in 1976.

Though Billy hasn't run our marathon since 1980 and doesn't win nearly as often anywhere anymore, he continues even today to be one of the most popular draws in the world. Every year we hassle each other about whether or not he's going to run New York, what his demands are, what I'm willing to give. Lately, I haven't been yielding. That's why he hasn't been running in New York.

When we decided to go "big" with our marathon in 1976, directing the course through all five boroughs, I knew we needed top names. My fear was that expanding the course to city-wide and the number of entrants to two thousand would not create enough excitement. We needed a couple of major runners to capture the attention of the press and public.

Obviously, the biggest name we could go after was Frank Shorter, who had won the Olympic gold medal in Munich in 1972 and the silver in Montreal in 1976.

Another name, new and not so big, but the one that would become the biggest of all, was Bill Rodgers.

I had never met him, although he had run the New York City Marathon in 1974, when I didn't even know who he was. He had been leading for most of that race, and after twenty miles this stranger was leading by a good half mile—running away from the field. Then he got hit by leg cramps. Crippled up, he managed to hang on and finish fifth. He was in such pain that he was immediately sent to the hospital. A few days later we got a letter from him. He apologized for not being able to show up at the awards ceremony.

But in 1975 Billy really burst onto the scene by winning the Boston Marathon in an American-record time of 2:09:55. He finished second to Shorter in the U.S. Olympic trials in 1976 but had a disastrous race in the subsequent Montreal Olympics; a foot injury had disrupted his training, and he finished fortieth.

Clearly, though, he was going to be a name to reckon with in coming years.

So I wanted Shorter and Rodgers for our first really big marathon.

I met Billy in August 1976 at the Falmouth 7-Mile Road Race on Cape Cod. I asked him to run New York in the coming October. He was very friendly and full of praise for our race, and readily agreed; he would be happy to run New York.

But an intermediary in charge of his business affairs and scheduling immediately stepped into the picture. If left to his own devices, Billy was so agreeable that he would say yes to everything and everybody. His intermediary could say no.

This person interceded and told me I would have to pay to get Billy for New York. It was the first time anybody had asked me for money. I guess maybe payments had gone on in small ways in other places, but it was no major factor that I had heard about. I assumed we might have to pick up expenses.

I asked how much. I was told two thousand dollars plus expenses. Two thousand just to guarantee his appearance. I was appalled. I couldn't believe the amount. The intermediary figured we needed Billy more than he needed us. Maybe that was right, at that point. In any event, I agreed.

We didn't have that kind of money at that time. But I like to gamble. I figured we could come up with it somehow. Our bookkeeping and budget procedures then were casual at best. We really didn't know how much anything was going to cost that first five-borough year. We had come up with some sponsorship and budgeted something like $25,000 for the whole event—without considering having to pay runners. Even if the money for Rodgers came out of my own pocket, I thought it would be a good investment. I anticipated all manner of possible problems in a race that went through the entire city, good neighborhoods and bad. But the best shot we had at success was to put on a good show and draw attention to it.

I contacted Shorter, who also agreed to come, and we treated him fairly.

In those days I was not taking a salary at the Road Runners Club. I was working in the Garment District making pretty good money and had been able to stash some away. I would need it.

Brian Crawford, then treasurer of the Road Runners, was a longtime friend of mine. That was very convenient because we were going to have to make some considerable off-the-books transactions. Back then, there were not all the various guises and subterfuges that later evolved by which money could be channeled to amateur runners—or at least we didn't know about them. Everything was truly under the table, cash.

Brian was the "bagman," as we like to joke. It wasn't such a joke at the time because the bag had quite a bit of cash in it. Shortly before the marathon Brian went to Billy's hotel room and gave him two thousand dollars.

The money came out of my own pocket. But we had our stars. And I never regretted a penny of it because the 1976 marathon launched us into the big time, right on the crest of the running boom.

Shorter was the favorite, and I picked him to win. But Rodgers won, in a fine time of 2:10:10, beating Shorter by two minutes. We got big crowds and great press. The worst thing that happened was that Billy's car, which had been illegally parked, was towed away by the police. But even that provided a nice twist of publicity, and we picked up the towing charges.

Billy became an instant celebrity, very marketable. Everybody loved him. Everybody wanted him for races all over the place—everything from 10-Ks to marathons. He won or placed near the top consistently. Within a few months he was able to open the first of a chain of running-gear stores in Boston, emulating Shorter's enterprises in Boulder, Colorado.

In 1977 our marathon more than doubled in size. We extended our "appearance" money to cover other runners, foreigners little known here whom we wanted for a strong international flavor. Billy felt the pressure in defending his title here, and although he was very serious and very nervous, he won again, easily beating Canada's Jerome Drayton by two and a half minutes. He further endeared himself to the crowd by typically deferring praise in behalf of lesser runners. Right after his win, he was on the VIP platform receiving congratulations while the middle-of-the-pack runners were still flooding across the finish line. He said, "Thanks," then immediately added, "But now let's give our attention to the other runners coming in."

For his performances in 1977 he was voted best marathoner in the world by *Runner's World* magazine and *Track & Field News*.

In 1978 we doubled in size again, accepting 11,218 entrants. And for a third straight time Billy won, clocking 2:12:12 and beating Britain's Ian Thompson by two minutes.

As marathoning leaped in public interest, we realized we had a true world-class sports hero on our hands. He seemed to be running in more and more races—10-Ks, 10-milers, marathons. In 1978, Billy said, he ran in thirty-five of the two hundred races he had been invited to. For a long-distance runner that is a huge number of races.

In April 1979 he broke his own American record in Boston with a time of 2:09:27, twenty-eight seconds under his 1975 mark. His marketability was soaring, and he was taking advantage of it. For example, during 1979 Perrier, one of our early marathon sponsors, held a series of 10-kilometer races around the country (including New York). The races included a highly publicized lottery, the winners to get a trip to France and Monte Carlo. As an added lure, Perrier hired Rodgers to be the celebrity host for the trip.

While Billy was riding so high, he began to bad-mouth me and the New York City Marathon. His price had been going up every year, and every year we were getting bigger, too. And because of our growing status, we were being more selective. There were new runners coming along. Everything was getting more competitive. We were backing off the idea of paying "appearance" money and instituting instead a prize-money structure (still under the table) for top finishers. We didn't need to beg anybody to run New York anymore and felt we should pay them on merit—on how they performed here. We were, simply, in a better negotiating position, and so we were negotiating.

I don't know whether his public anti-Lebow statements were

part of his negotiating strategy, or just Billy being outspoken about what he believed, or a combination of the two, or what. But, for example, during the summer before our 1979 marathon he told an interviewer: "New York is being very cheap. They don't know if they want to cover my travel expenses, they don't know who they want to invite. They're being very snobby."

As for us being "cheap," at that time we gave more money than any other marathon in the country, and Billy was being a bit disingenuous in speaking of "travel expenses" when what he meant was money beyond that. We knew enough about how fast the sport was developing to be aware that runners nobody had heard of yet were likely to emerge out of nowhere as new stars. That's why it was becoming so competitive.

In that same interview Billy admitted: "I would prefer to go to New York than Fukuoka" (Japan, six weeks after New York). "New York is better publicity, which would help my clothing business. That's how I make my living."

More and more, of course, he was adding to that living with his escalating, hidden running fees—although the scales hadn't yet tipped as dramatically as they would in the next year or two. But, yes, New York is better publicity than Fukuoka—New York gets more publicity than any other marathon—even though the Fukuoka race, an elite invitational, is one of the world's most prestigious marathons.

As for the New York City Marathon, Billy predicted: "There will never be a world record there. There's no one walking the earth now that can run 2:08:34 in New York." (That was the existing world record.) "It's not very hilly, but it has very uneven surfaces, like potholes, and there's a lot of turns. No one has ever broken 2:13 on that course, except myself."

The prediction turned out to be wrong (Alberto Salazar, who would break the world record in New York in 1981, was then "walking the earth"). Although I might have held out for better bargains, I never reneged on anything, always delivered what I promised, always did my best to take care of runners who came. I continued to deal with Billy, and he continued to come to New York to race—even that same year, 1979.

That time I was already annoyed when he got here. Just two weeks before, he had run a serious marathon in Toronto. He got a big fee for it. Nobody can give two topflight marathon performances in two weeks. As a responsible person, he had an obligation to come here in good shape, not tired.

Well, he won again, and he was a bigger hero than ever. *Sports Illustrated* put him on the cover, with the headline "FOUR IN A ROW!" Bloomingdale's department store sold out on Bill Rodgers running clothes.

Then he told a TV interviewer that he wouldn't come back to New York again unless we treated runners better. Billy knew that we treated invited runners like himself better than any other marathon did. He was truly the king of the New York City Marathon, the darling of the press and the fans, and, I must say, still a favorite of mine.

But I was nagged by the fact that his winning time—2:11:42—although good, was not as good as it might have been. For what we had been giving him, directly and indirectly, we deserved his best effort, not just his best effort after having run a race somewhere else. Maybe even *he* had a world record in him if he hadn't overextended himself.

In 1980 I had some sympathy for Billy. He had really been priming for the Olympics in Moscow. At thirty-two he felt it would be his last best shot at a gold medal, and he figured rightly that an Olympic gold, with all its glamour and publicity and maybe even TV work (to which he had long aspired), could set him up for life. He was ready to peak in Moscow for perhaps the best effort of his life. Then the United States boycotted the Olympics.

He wanted to come to New York to defend his crown. We had the usual wrangling. We wouldn't give him any appearance money, but we did our best to accommodate him in other ways to compensate. We bought dozens of sets of his Bill Rodgers running suits. We set up some personal appearances—such as clinics during pre-race week—for which sponsors would pay him a fee. There was also the chance of prize money if he finished near the top.

So he ran. Wearing his familiar Snoopy stocking cap and white cotton gloves, Billy was running a good race, in the midst of the lead pack, for fourteen miles. Then a runner behind him stepped on his heel and caused him to fall. He recovered quickly and pushed gamely to finish fifth.

The crowd at the finish line had heard about his fall and was waiting for him. They cheered as loudly for him as they had for the winner, Alberto Salazar (then one of those new stars, who was running his first marathon). Billy was still everybody's favorite.

Even without the Olympic gold it was not a bad year. Billy later revealed that he had made $250,000 in business, clinics, and racing (an amount that would more than double in the next couple of years).

In 1981 things really heated up about the secret prize-money business. More and more stories were appearing in the press, speculating about how much was being paid and to whom. It seemed that a full-fledged scandal could break at any time.

We were working behind the scenes with The Athletics Congress (TAC) to come up with some form of above-board payments that might be channeled through that governing body. Meanwhile, some runners, including Rodgers, impatient with official progress, decided to tackle the issue on their own. They formed a group called the Association of Road Racing Athletes (ARRA), whose members participated in a handful of races with straightforward cash payments. I opposed that, preferring to come up with a solution through TAC that would protect everybody. Some of the runners who took money in the ARRA races were banned from TAC-sanctioned races for a while. Billy was not one of them. He had run in the races but apparently had not taken the prize money. (There were some runners who, while supporting ARRA by participation, still didn't want to jeopardize their amateur standing.)

Subsequently, there was a hassle about his running the Stockholm Marathon, and it seems he thought I was responsible because of my opposition to his ARRA participation. But I had nothing to do with it. What might have had a *lot* to do with it was the fee he was asking. I heard it was thirty thousand.

Through these years we had pretty much been giving in to his business representative on Billy's demands. I would be told: "Billy deserves a lot because he made the New York Marathon what it is." Well, I thought the reverse was just as true. We benefited from one another. He felt he deserved more respect than we gave him, and I felt we deserved more respect than he gave us. Maybe one thing that rankled with him was that I had never picked Billy to win in New York. Not once. (I used to pick Shorter to win.) But I thought it was a good-natured bone of contention between us. Billy knew that I respected him as a runner and as a decent, honest guy. He often confided in me, and I respected that.

He knew that I always wanted him to run in New York and that I bent a lot to his wishes. But now he wasn't the defending champion anymore. I said publicly that although he was still the best known and most popular marathoner in the world, I didn't think he would ever again win the New York City Marathon.

If he didn't come in 1981, I figured he'd be the real loser, not us. Still, I wanted him. He was good for publicity, he was still a premier runner, he was still a favorite. I liked having him around. He added sparkle.

But now he was represented by a big-time agency, International Management Group, which handled some of the best known athletes in the world, including many top runners. IMG was trying to pressure me to make a deal with Billy.

I didn't like how they were pushing me—or him. I thought they were urging him to take too many races just for the dollars. By running too much I thought Billy would be prematurely burned out. Since I felt that Billy needed us more than we needed him, I adopted a strategy that I often do—I did nothing. I was noncommittal. I chatted with Billy occasionally, always managing to mention the value of running New York, but basically I just let the time go by, let the marathon approach, figuring he'd come around. I let the press speculate whether we were feuding again. That never hurt. Every time they mentioned our feud, they mentioned our marathon.

Then, like 1979 all over again, Billy decided to run another marathon just two weeks before ours—the Bank One Marathon in Columbus, Ohio. I couldn't believe it. If you have any serious intentions about New York, running *any* marathon two weeks beforehand is foolish. And to run a *minor* one is ludicrous. It cannot enhance your prestige.

I went out to Columbus to run the marathon myself, check out the scene, and see where Billy's head was. He finished seventh. He was still interested in coming to New York.

We managed to work out a deal that wouldn't cost me anything and would benefit him: I would get him some sponsors. And I did. We got Perrier and the New York investment firm of Rooney Pace to sponsor him. In return, he had to do some promotion, and he had to wear their names on his running clothes in the marathon.

It turned out to be one of the more bizarre debacles I've seen around a marathon.

I was not involved in the haggling, but apparently they dickered about money right down to the wire, resolving the issue the day before the marathon. Then it seems that Billy was not happy about sponsors' names adorning his racing clothes like an Indianapolis race-car driver. Finally that, too, was settled: "Perrier" would be on the front of his shirt, the Rooney Pace logo on the back of his shorts.

When the finished clothes were delivered to Billy in his hotel, the logo was also on the *front* of his shorts, and Billy rebelled.

I didn't know this was going on. The day and night before the marathon are insanely busy, and I had put the Rodgers matter out of my mind. I assumed everything was okay. Everything was certainly okay between Billy and me.

About 7 or 8 P.M. I left our marathon headquarters at the Sheraton Centre Hotel to go to the finish line in Central Park, where there is always a lot of last-minute preparation that takes us all night. I ran into Billy's girl friend (now his wife), Gail. She was very upset. She said, "Fred, they're still negotiating up there, and it's driving me crazy. I had to leave the room because I couldn't stand the arguing."

I couldn't believe it. The night before the marathon, when he should be relaxing, Billy's up there in his hotel room arguing over a sponsor. That was demeaning to him. I said to Gail: "Why don't you go back there and tell Billy to tell them to go to hell—all of them, agents, sponsors, everybody. Let him just go ahead and run the marathon. Then he and I can work something out afterward."

Sometime during the middle of the night, Billy ended the argument. The combination of haggling with sponsors and not being fit to run a good race led him to a decision. He wouldn't run wearing the sponsors' names; he wouldn't run the marathon at all.

I didn't even know Billy wasn't in the race until after it had started, when I heard it over the radio in the lead car.

It turned out to be the greatest race ever because Alberto Salazar set a men's world record—right there where Billy had said it was impossible—and Allison Roe set a women's world record.

After all that, I didn't approach Billy to run in New York in 1982. Now claiming world's records for both men and women, we were on top of the world. We were getting more media attention than ever.

Not all of it was positive, though. I became a target of some who seemed to feel I was some kind of charlatan, that all this success must be attributable to cynical, sinister maneuvering by Fred Lebow. And one of the favorite people to quote in that vein was Bill Rodgers.

In the September issue of a magazine called *Running* (not to be confused with *The Runner, Runners World,* or even our own magazine, *New York Running News*) Billy had this to say about me: "Fred knows next to nothing about running. But because he's dealing with sponsors who know *absolutely* nothing about running, he has himself in a kind of guru position. They come to him, and they do what he says. His entire success is based on the fact that he deals with people, sponsors, who know nothing about the sport. I've built the [New York City Marathon] as much as anyone, and Lebow . . . treats all of us in a very condescending way. . . . He likes to have power over runners. . . . I think he gets off by stepping on world-class runners."

Well, sometimes I think maybe Billy gets off by stepping on Fred Lebow. We're still friendly in private, but when somebody puts a mike in front of him, he can't resist being negative about me.

After that article came out, Billy called me (collect as usual—a holdover from his earlier years when he didn't have any money and I invited him to call collect, a practice I haven't discouraged since) and said that they had used old quotes, taken out of context. It was thoughtful of him to call. I always enjoy his calls, when he is talking only to me.

In fact, through all this time, through all the public bickering and nonsense about feuds and all that, Billy and I continued to spend warm, friendly times together. We were both in Miami for the Orange Bowl Marathon a couple of years ago, and we were sitting together in his hotel room watching a professional football play-off game on television. A fight broke out on the field, and one player threw his helmet at another. The crowd ate it up, fans jumping to their feet yelling and screaming and cheering.

Billy is truly a nonviolent type, but he recognized what brought the crowd alive. "The trouble with our sport of running, Fred," he said, "is that everybody loves everybody. But here the fans love it when somebody throws a helmet at somebody else."

It was typical of Billy's attitude—and even applies to the matter of money: Fans and sponsors alike ought to be able to respond as positively to such a peaceful, noncombatant sport like road racing with the same fervor they express for a fight on a football field.

In the summer of 1982 another runner told me that Billy was in excellent shape and was really anxious to run New York that year but was waiting for me to make some overtures. Whatever shape he was in, he could not beat Salazar—unless Salazar had a bad day and Billy had a great one, which was always a slight possibility.

Billy hadn't been running great times lately because, in my opinion, he hadn't been motivated. He was running too many marathons. He didn't have to run a great time to win a race in many parts of the world. But in New York he would have to run a great time to win. And here he might be motivated. But that was up to him.

He decided to pass up New York in 1982 and run the Big M marathon in Melbourne, Australia, just prior to New York, instead, where they were paying him a fee and had a much smaller field and weaker competition. He won, in a time that would have placed him third in New York.

A major change had taken place in the business of running in 1982. An international agreement had finally been worked out to allow open prize money. Races could pay a cash purse, which would go into a trust fund administered by each national governing body. In the United States it was TAC. The athlete who won the money could draw from his trust fund for "training expenses" (which were loosely defined), and the athlete's "amateur" status would be preserved.

But because of local complications (which I will go into later), we still couldn't do it in New York. We were caught in a squeeze. For the marathon to be legitimate under international rules, it had to be sanctioned by TAC. Under the new rules, in order to sanction a race, TAC had to approve the prize-money structure— if you gave prize money.

Theoretically, you didn't have to give prize money. Realistically, you did in order to attract a decent field of runners. In 1982 it was a kind of open secret with TAC that we paid, but we had to deny it publicly (or at least finesse it to avoid outright lying) and were allowed to get away with it because of our special circumstances.

But it was not a comfortable position to be in. And in 1983 one other marathon in particular was determined to make our position as uncomfortable as possible—Chicago. The Chicago race (which bills itself "America's Marathon"), held in October a week before New York, had decided to challenge us openly for elite runners and prestige. They publicized an enormous budget of $1.5 million—bigger than ours, for a field only half as large. And they published a prize-money structure totaling $135,000, daring us to do the same.

We still could not admit anything, and that put TAC in a difficult position as well. TAC knew about our prize money because we had to submit our plan to them in order to get their sanction. Chicago knew that; the whole running community knew that. But only TAC knew the actual numbers. TAC was sympathetic to our situation, and we managed once again—just barely—to get away with a semiconfidential agreement with TAC.

Bill Rodgers was one of the runners Chicago was bidding for.

Off and on through the summer of 1983 Billy and I discussed the possibility of his running New York. But he decided to run the Peking, China, Marathon in September. Now, if he gave Peking an all-out effort, he wouldn't be ready to run New York, anyway, just a month later. But I suggested to him that he could run easily in Peking and save himself for New York—and maybe even win Peking because the field wasn't awesome. And if he *could* win Peking without killing himself, well, then, his stock would be up and we might be able to work out something for New York.

In Peking the temperature at race time was near 90 degrees, and hot weather is a killer for Billy. He had to drop out a couple of miles before the finish.

Indications were he would try to run another marathon that same fall. That could be New York. Then all of a sudden, in early October, he announced that he was going to run the Chicago Marathon, and not New York. And the reason he wasn't going to run New York, he said, was Fred Lebow.

I heard another reason: $20,000. Not prize money. Chicago, I was informed by his agent, was bidding for Billy with a guarantee of $20,000 in appearance money.

The Chicago Marathon is an interesting case. It is not put on by a local running organization, as is the case in Boston, New York, and other places. It is directed by a man named Bob Bright, imported from New York and paid by the marathon's sponsor, Beatrice Foods. Bright is smart, tough, and ambitious. In 1980 he put on a 20-K race in Midlands, New Jersey. Not only was it to be a rich and high-budgeted race, but Bright guaranteed that invited Russian runners would come—which would then have been a first for any road race in the United States.

It was a fiasco. The money didn't turn up, and neither did the Russians. Bright had guaranteed Bill Rodgers $5,000, but there was no money to pay him that guarantee.

Coincidentally, I had to go to Chicago about ten days before the Chicago Marathon to be an observer at a smaller women's race put on by a sponsor we work with. I called Bright to tell him I was coming. (As I do with most race directors—even those trying to be competitive with us—I maintain a cordial relationship with Bright.) I told him I had heard that he had offered Billy between $15,000 and $25,000. He wanted to know what *I* was offering Billy. I said that I had let it be known that if Billy ran New York and did well, I would take care of him, but had not mentioned a dollar figure. Bright suggested that when I came out to Chicago, in a couple of days, we should have dinner.

Then I talked to Billy's agent. The agent confirmed the $20,000 bid from Chicago and said that if I would match it, Billy would run New York instead. Billy, he said, was truly upset with me because I hadn't approached him.

"When it comes to me," I said, "sometimes Billy's just not rational. Are you telling me that money is the only thing that would fix this up? I can't believe it."

That's the way it is, he said.

"Well," I said, "if you were me, what would you do? He would benefit more from a tenth-place finish in New York than second or third in Chicago."

His advice was to match Chicago's offer.

"I have mixed feelings," I said. "On the one hand, I'm angry, I feel like saying, 'To hell with you, Billy, go to Chicago.' On the other hand, for sentimental reasons, it would be nice to have him run New York. But there's also the principle involved, believe it or not. We've been very good to him. We're not getting into a bidding war with anybody, least of all Chicago."

The agent said he needed an answer today. I said, "I'm not going to say no right now. I want to think about it, talk it over with a couple of people."

I thought the agent was maybe trying to play Bright and me off each other, and I resented having anybody even *think* they could do that. Because we were in a squeeze about open prize money, maybe some people thought we were vulnerable to pressure, or even that we would be forced to compete with Chicago to maintain our position in the marathon world.

Chicago wasn't in our league. They had 8,000 runners, compared to our 17,000. No matter what Chicago paid, even if they seduced a runner or two from us, they couldn't duplicate the overall quality of our race—the size and excitement of our field, the city and volunteer support, the network TV and mass of publicity, the care and handling we give everybody.

By challenging us, trying to stir us up, Bright was getting some attention from the press. But a bidding war, or even talk of it, could only help Chicago, and I wasn't about to fall for this.

Since there were only a few days before the Chicago Marathon, they needed Billy right away. For him to be of value, they had to have time to promote him as an entrant. They couldn't publicly claim him until they were sure I wasn't going to get him. And if they couldn't claim him, they couldn't promote him.

There was no way I was going to match Chicago's bid. But the longer I delayed in saying so, the less time Chicago would have. So I would keep Bright, Billy, and the agent dangling on a string as long as I could before giving my answer.

About the same time, I was informed by people in New York who were organizing a sports medicine clinic as part of our marathon-week events that Billy had volunteered his services. I couldn't believe it! Billy is passing up our race in favor of Chicago, and yet he's coming to New York to do a clinic for us, for *free!*

As always, he was a mass of paradoxes. I couldn't resist calling him. He was his usual friendly self. I teased him about the "good press" he was giving us and wished him well in Chicago. Sincerely, I thanked him for offering to do the free clinic for us. And just to show I wasn't such a bad guy, I made him an offer—not for New York, but for Jamaica. We were helping organize a 10-K race in Jamaica for January, and I told him I was pretty sure I could get him $5,000 to run in it. It would be a nice trip for you and your new wife, I told him. He thought that was a nice idea, and he would think it over.

I flew to Chicago as planned, arriving on a warm, sunny afternoon. I decided to take a short run along the Lake Michigan shore, then maybe catch a nap, before having dinner with Bob Bright.

After my run, I lay down in a grassy area among some sunbathers. I took off my running shoes and fell asleep. When I woke up, my shoes were gone. I looked everywhere, even the trash cans. I had to walk a mile back to my hotel in my white socks.

Who would want a pair of old, smelly running shoes? I had been running near the hotel where Bright stayed. Maybe he had happened by and taken them, as a joke. It wouldn't be unlike him.

At dinner Bright denied taking my running shoes. But he admitted he was paying Billy $20,000. I admitted I wasn't making an offer.

My delaying tactics worked. By the time he could put the word out that Billy would run Chicago, the papers only ran a little blurb about it.

Back in August, just two months before he chose to run Chicago instead of New York, Billy had come, at my invitation, to open our lottery drawing on the steps of City Hall. (We take the first half of our field first-come, first-served, then finish the field by lottery.) Standing on the steps with Mayor Koch, a bunch of dignitaries, and me, in front of all the TV cameras, Billy proclaimed: "Clearly, the New York City Marathon is the most important big-city marathon in the world."

When he subsequently went to Chicago, he said, "The Chicago Marathon is the best marathon of the fall."

So he ran the Chicago Marathon. He finished a woeful twenty-seventh. I was glad he hadn't opted for New York. But I missed him.

3

Since 1981 the New York Road Runners Club has owned its own building, a narrow, six-story, forty-room stone structure, a nineteenth-century family mansion, in a neighborhood of classy residential apartment buildings on East 89th Street, near Fifth Avenue, in New York. We call it the International Running Center. I don't know of any other running organization that has such substantial offices. Prior to moving into this building, the Road Runners Club was cramped into a few small rented rooms in the West Side YMCA. How we came to own this building is a story I will tell later.

Two stories above the sidewalk hangs our eight-by-four-foot banner; on a light blue field are the words "New York Road Runners Club—International Running Center." In the middle is the club's logo: a bright red apple enclosing a white triangle in which is a silhouetted running figure and the letters "RRC."

The glass front doors are covered by heavy, ornate, wrought-iron grillwork. The lobby, like most of the building, is carpeted. To the right as you enter is the receptionist's desk with its push-button bank of telephones—hub of the club's fifty-unit system that allows intricate switching and paging. To the left is the merchandise counter behind which, covering the wall, are displays of the club's running gear—T-shirts, warm-ups, bags, caps.

The whole place is pleasant and comfortable, but primarily casual. The lobby is a hive where runners gather, chat, get information, pick up entry blanks for races. Unless one knows who is who, it is difficult to tell the staff from the crowd, since everyone is a runner, and everyone dresses in running clothes.

Straight ahead to the rear is the Albert H. Gordon Library, crammed with running books, running magazines from around the world, computerized files of clippings, historical matter, all kinds of data. It is named for the chairman of the board of Kidder, Peabody, the prominent stock brokerage firm. Gordon recently contributed several thousand dollars for computerization of the library.

On the second floor are three large rooms where meetings, exercise clinics, race registration, exhibits, and parties are held.

The upper floors are for the staff offices. The third floor houses people involved with race organization and direction, volunteer coordination, and handling of elite athletes. Major computer operations are on the fifth floor, magazine production on the sixth. *The New York Running News* is a slick, four-color publication we put out every other month, containing, in addition to articles, results of every NYRRC race.

The fourth floor houses the large office of the controller and his staff in front, a kitchen, the office of our vice-president and my right-hand man, Allan Steinfeld, and my spacious room in the rear.

My office, airy and comfortable, with high ceilings, is as informal as the rest of the place and furnished for utility. I am not concerned with trappings, except for what is needed to suggest a little dignity for the business we transact there.

In front of my desk are a few black armchairs for meetings. A sofa is against the opposite wall. Large photographs and paintings of running scenes are on the walls. Various awards and citations we have collected over the years are scattered here and there. There is a computer terminal, a telex, a decorative fireplace, an air conditioner. Near my desk is the desk of my assistant, Debbie Ulian, who manages to keep the room and my desk reasonably tidy (I tend to scatter things and lose stuff). On my desk are two beige telephones which ring continually.

Overall the building is not plush. Most of the offices are small and crowded, and as more people come aboard, new cubbyholes have to be found or hollowed out.

Running clothes are what most of the staff wear most of the time, and in the office they are what I wear all of the time. But now I also have in my closet a couple of jackets and ties because I am called on to attend banquets and meetings with people in business, government, and sport, for which I must dress more formally. In another walk-around closet there are drawers and shelves overflowing with running clothes, all of which are provided by manufacturers and suppliers.

My days are busy with talk: meetings, interviews, telephones. I don't have a routine. The IRC may open officially at 9 or 10 and close at 6 or 9 P.M., depending on the season and the crush of events. But my days have no standard beginning or end. There are things written on my desk calendar, but that is not a reliable guide to my schedule. Things keep coming up, and I pretty much take them as they come. I am most often reminded of appointments either by people showing up for them or by staff who tell me I'm due someplace.

Here's a day taken at random: Intending to be in my office at nine, I am delayed at a breakfast meeting with a magazine editor. Then, unable to get a cab in the pouring rain, I run three miles to arrive sopping wet at ten o'clock. I change from my wet warmup suit to a dry one and put on a T-shirt on which is lettered "ROMARATONA," a souvenir from the Rome Marathon I recently ran.

My first appointment was supposed to be at 9:30. I don't remember making the appointment or whom it is with or what it is for. But I'm told there is a woman who has been waiting for an hour down in the lobby, and I send for her. She is pretty, with long, curly black hair, a white minidress, black boots. She says she is a part-time actress trying to build a party-producing business. She wants to put on our big postmarathon disco party for the runners. I tell her what's needed—big space, food and drink, decorations, music. She is eager to do it, and I ask her to send me a proposal.

I already have someone to put on that party, but she seemed smart and I wanted her credentials checked out and I wanted to see how she put together a proposal; you never know when you might need someone with enthusiasm and brains to work with.

Staff members pop in one after the other. One has a problem with an advertiser in our magazine. Another is concerned about some conflicts involving foreign runners. Another wants to discuss a phase of the planning for the upcoming World Cross Country Championships, which will be held in the United States for the first time, hosted by the NYRRC.

I have a lunch date with Ollan Cassell, executive director of TAC, at the New York Athletic Club at one o'clock. At least my calendar says one o'clock. At 12:30 somebody calls from the NYAC to tell me I'm late for lunch. I scramble around to change into a jacket and tie and slacks. I can't find matching socks, so I'll try to get away with one brown one and one black. The NYAC requires a tie and jacket. Once I went there for a lunch with Cassell, and I had on a tie and jacket, but I was wearing running shoes. They wouldn't let me in. Cassell took me around the corner and bought me a pair of dress shoes so I could get into his club for lunch. This time I am wearing dress shoes.

At the lunch we discuss prize money and TAC sanctions for upcoming events.

I arrive back at my office an hour late for a two o'clock meeting with men from a sportswear company that is the official outfitter for the upcoming marathon. They will provide 20,000 T-shirts for the runners, 1,500 rain suits for NYRRC course officials. We discuss design, sizes, colors, delivery dates.

I hurry out to catch a cab for Brooklyn, where, at a YWCA, I address some local people on the values of the NYRRC's Urban Running Program, a new activity for inner-city youngsters, and on plans for the Brooklyn Half Marathon.

At 8:30 P.M. there is a board of directors meeting. I bring the members up to date on budget matters and events.

At 10 P.M. I have dinner with some investment bankers for preliminary discussion of possible sponsorship of some events, such as the first New York Triathalon and the 6-Day Run.

Ordinarily, I try to work in a late-hour run of five or six miles. Sometimes I will even run at midnight. This night, however, I decide to meet a lady at a disco for a drink instead.

In my office concentration is a problem (that's why I do a lot of my thinking while I run). When an interview or a meeting begins to drag, I sometimes find myself skimming magazines or newspapers. If the phone rings and nobody else answers it, I will answer it. I never let a phone just ring. One of my unfortunate traits is that I allow interruptions during meetings. Staff members gripe about not getting me to concentrate on whatever problems they want to discuss, because there are always interruptions.

When there is no talk—no telephones, no meetings—I have trouble sitting still. So when my office is empty, I usually leave it to roam around the building and see what everybody is doing.

There are always many projects going on at once. There are races virtually every weekend, and sometimes a couple at the same time in different places. Responsibility for directing them is spread around. For the major events, planning for volunteers, sponsors, logistics, invited runners is begun months ahead of time. Work is proceeding on the Perrier 10-K run and the Trevira Twosome, a 10-mile race for couples; on the L'eggs Mini Marathon, a 10-K race for women; on the 13.1-mile Westchester Half Marathon and the 10-K Pepsi Challenge National Championships.

Some people are working on the ultramarathons (distances beyond the 26.2-mile marathon), such as the 100-Mile Run and the 6-Day Run; others are organizing the Manufacturers Hanover Trust Corporate Challenge, a series of 3.5-mile races for corporate teams. There is the 5th Avenue Mile and the Empire State Building Run-Up (1,575 stairs, 86 stories) and the New York City Triathlon (2-kilometer swim from the Statue of Liberty to Battery Park on the southern tip of Manhattan, 38-K bike race around Manhattan to Central Park, 10-K footrace in Central Park). Work has been going on for years to prepare for hosting the 1984 World Cross Country Championships at the Meadowlands racetrack in East Rutherford, New Jersey. There is the Urban Running Program to direct and the Riker's Island Olympics for prisoners, at New York's maximum-security prison.

Interspersed with all these are the dozens of smaller races, each requiring staffing of organizers, directors, officials, volunteers. And there are the demands for staff to observe, consult, or direct road races elsewhere in the world. Add to that the functions of merchandising, magazine production, press and public relations, exhibitions, art shows, clinics—and all the time, throughout the year, there is work to be done on the main marathon. It is a busy staff.

Our staff is mostly young—at least judging it from my perspective of fifty-two years. Most are in their twenties and thirties, the majority are single, about half are women. Virtually everybody runs. They're given a pretty free rein to develop their areas, expand their roles, take a lot of responsibility. They work long hours and they work weekends because that's when the races are. They grouse some about that, but they seem to enjoy it. If they didn't, they probably wouldn't be there because we don't pay much.

They are all from other businesses—which is natural enough, because this business didn't exist for anybody a few years ago. Typically, they get involved as volunteers. Some of the volunteers get paid a per diem for certain demanding events, like the marathon. And some of them eventually get hired. But we have several people practically full-time who are still volunteers. It's a motley group. We have lawyers, teachers, people from the business world and banking, people from the theater and the post office and politics. Most of them left better-paying jobs, and most of them could earn two or three times as much someplace else. I didn't take a salary until 1982. Now I am paid $30,000 a year. A couple of people make more, but most make a good deal less. The dedication we get from volunteers and staff is enormous, and I don't think it's duplicated anywhere else.

In the early days of my administration, when there were few races and few staff, I knew what everybody was doing all the time. Now I don't. I don't need to. The primary reason for that is the presence of Allan Steinfeld, my second-in-command. Allan is on top of everything, in a class by himself, the preeminent technical genius in road racing.

Steinfeld, at thirty-eight, is still lean as a sprinter—which he was in his college days when he ran the quarter- and half-mile. He has a mop of dark curly hair and a beard. A native New Yorker, he earned degrees in electrical engineering and physics and was a Ph.D. candidate in radio astronomy when he left the higher levels of academia. Before joining the NYRRC, he taught math and physics, and was track coach, at a suburban high school.

Allan is given less public attention than he deserves. It's not only I who recognize him as a genius. Inside the running world and throughout the official running world he is known as the consummate master of the crafting of road races. And even in track and field he has acknowledged expertise as a race official. I think he'll be the next long-distance running chairman of The Athletics Congress. And my guess is that eventually he'll be a major power in the International Amateur Athletic Federation and even the International Olympic Committee. At the 1984 Olympics he was chief referee for the men's and women's marathons, with overall responsibility for rules (I was special adviser to the director).

When it comes to timing, scoring, measuring courses, designing finish-line systems, radio communications, tying everything together with computers, there is nobody anywhere like Allan. I never pretended to know all that much about those areas. If I didn't have Allan, I might have been forced to educate myself about them. But since he's around, I don't have to worry about such things. (I only have to worry about keeping him. In 1983 there was a serious attempt to hire him away, to direct a corporate running program for a lot more money. I'll discuss that later.)

Allan's strength is not just in technical areas, as it once was. As he's evolved, he's developed tremendous rapport with sponsors, government officials, everybody. He's great with the staff. People are amazed at how different we are, different in just about every respect. But we complement each other. In the eight years we've known each other, we've rarely had a serious disagreement. (I did get angry with him once, and that was in the unlikely matter of a love triangle that threatened to interfere with the marathon; more on that later, too.)

We may not always agree on day-to-day operations, but we definitely agree on the basic goals and purposes, the long-range plan, where we're headed. Much of the success of the club and our marathon can be credited to Allan. And whenever I decide to step down—or I'm deposed—Allan's the only one I can see taking over this position, both as director of the New York City Marathon and as president of the New York Road Runners Club.

I wish I'd had him in the beginning. But he didn't come along until 1976, and that was in the nick of time.

Before I ran, the only sport I ever really got involved in was tennis. I never got very good, but I was extremely competitive. I couldn't stand to lose. In the 1960s I played a lot with my buddy Brian Crawford, with whom I shared an apartment. He beat me all the time. And since I couldn't stand to lose, I got very depressed about it. I got so unreasonably depressed that I considered seeing a shrink.

The coach at the Midtown Tennis Club said my trouble was that I needed to build up my strength and stamina. I joined a health club. For a couple of weeks I lifted weights. I was bored stiff. The man at the health club said that if weight training was not for me, I should try jogging. He recommended the path around the reservoir in the middle of Central Park.

The first time, I went with Brian, and we took a couple of dates as a kind of audience. Because, as usual, it was a competition. We bet a couple of dollars who would finish the loop first. One time around was just over a mile and a half. Brian, who was heavier than I, had to stop after a mile. I kept going and finished. Most important was that I beat Brian. Second most important was that I ran that distance without stopping, which was a big success and very exhilarating. It was an entirely new kind of feeling—to run.

I never lost another tennis match because I never played another tennis match. From then on, every chance I got, I would go to the reservoir to run, by myself. It was such a wonderful feeling of freedom, an outlet for pent-up energy, like maybe a horse that's been kept in a stall for a year and then is finally let free.

In those days I was working for a textile company and was extremely diligent about work. I would go in early and leave late, and never miss a day. But there was one day when I looked out the window and saw how sunny and beautiful it was, and I just had to get out. At eleven o'clock I told my secretary I would be gone for a couple of hours. I went up to the reservoir and ran for a long time. I couldn't believe I was taking time off from work to do that, but that's how strong my feeling for running was. It was taking me over.

I remember thinking: What is it that I've suddenly discovered? Am I the only one who feels this way? Is there something wrong with me? Because I hardly ever saw anyone else running.

At a big corner newsstand, which was well stocked and had just about everything, I tried to find a magazine about running. There were all kinds of magazines about sports—fishing, tennis, golf, basketball, football, baseball. I asked the guy for something about running. He was Greek and didn't understand right away. I said, "You know, running, like track." He gave me a magazine called *Road & Track*. The one about cars.

I went to the library and looked in the card catalog under "Running" and "Track." There was a book about improving your sprinting ability, so I took it out. Among the things I saw right away was that you had to have good running shoes.

At a sporting-goods store I asked for running shoes. The guy sold me a pair of Tretorns, leather shoes made in Sweden that he said were the hottest new item. I ran in them for a while. They were heavy and hot. I found out they were actually tennis shoes. I went back to the store and told the guy that I was supposed to have shoes that were very light and flexible, specifically for running. The guy said, "Oh, you want spikes. What length spikes do you want?" Whatever is best, I said.

So I bought a pair of spiked shoes, the kind sprinters use on tracks. It made sense to me. On the dirt path around the reservoir they were fine. But in running to and from the reservoir, along the city streets, the spikes made a clatter that drew a lot of unwanted attention to me, and they hurt my feet when I ran on concrete.

One day I got into conversation with another jogger at the reservoir, and he said he ran in road races. I said I would like to try that. He said there was a race coming up, a 5-miler—eleven laps around Yankee Stadium in the Bronx. He also told me I should get proper shoes and directed me at last to where I bought my first pair of actual road-running shoes, Adidas. (Also the last pair I ever bought, since I started getting them free from running-shoe companies.)

I went up to Yankee Stadium to run that race, and that was my first contact with the New York Road Runners Club. Actually, in those days it was just a local affiliation with the Road Runners Club of America and was called the RRCA, New York Association. There were a few dozen men there to race, and the race was divided into two sections, fast and slow. I entered the slow section. We went around and around Yankee Stadium. Everybody passed me. Everybody except one old guy, maybe sixty-five. I beat that one guy.

I've always felt since then that if I hadn't beaten that old guy, there wouldn't have ever been a New York City Marathon. Because if I had been dead last in my first race I would have been so discouraged that I would have given up running.

Right after that, in 1969, I joined the club for three dollars and entered all their races—there were just a handful, mostly cross-country races in Van Cortlandt Park, in the Bronx.

The club was a small clique of men who seemed reluctant to share their world with outsiders, which included me. They talked about running, and I was thirsty for any kind of information: Was I lifting my legs properly, moving my arms correctly, breathing right? But they were not very communicative to me, and the language they used among themselves in talking about running—language runners understand, about splits and pace and surging and drafting—was foreign to me.

But I persisted, because I loved the running.

That same group held a marathon each year. Called the Cherry Tree Marathon (because it was run on Washington's birthday), it was held on streets that wound around tenement buildings in the hilly vicinity of Yankee Stadium. I decided to run that marathon in 1970. I trained and trained to build up my mileage. The field was about sixty men. There were a few officials with stopwatches. As my first actual marathon of 26 miles 385 yards, it was exciting. I finished in four hours nine minutes.

But there were no spectators. Automobile traffic was difficult. Some kids threw stones. The surroundings were drab.

Running a marathon was great (I ran twelve more in the ensuing twelve months, wherever I could find them, including Boston). But afterward I thought: Why, in this big city of New York, is such a wonderful event relegated to some dreary streets in the Bronx? In beautiful Central Park, right in the heart of the city, there is a smooth, wide road that meanders among the rocks and trees in a loop of about six miles. Recently, Mayor John Lindsay had closed that road to automobile traffic on weekends. Why not hold the marathon there? I kept thinking about it.

Finally I verbalized my thoughts to some joggers I met while doing my training in Central Park. They thought it was a great idea. I imagined it would cost a few hundred dollars. I asked these people if they would help me sponsor a marathon in Central Park. They said they would be happy to help.

At the time, I didn't know my way about the world of long-distance running at all. I didn't know the personalities, the politics, the history. But right here in New York we had the foremost pioneers of American road running. People like Ted Corbitt, a former Olympian and the man called the father of American distance running; Aldo Scandurra, president of the Metropolitan Amateur Athletic Union; Joe Kleinerman, one of the chief organizers of road races and coach of the famed

Millrose Athletic Association track team; Kurt Steiner, onetime French Foreign Legionnaire and a race walker as well as a runner; other fine runners like Ben Malkasian and Vince Chiappetta. All these people have been heavily involved with our club ever since and have served as officers at one time or another. Corbitt, Scandurra, and Chiappetta served as presidents.

Until 1958 the only national outfit engaged with long-distance running in this country was the Amateur Athletic Union, then the governing body for track and field (until replaced by TAC, which was formed under the federal Amateur Sports Act of 1978), and not much was happening in the road-racing area. In England there was the Road Runners Club, which was very active. So in 1958 some prominent American runners met in New York to form a counterpart of the British organization. They called it the Road Runners Club of America. Soon after that, some of these local New York people formed the RRCA, New York Association. It had forty-two members. They elected Ted Corbitt, the most prominent among them, as the first president.

At first the local division of the AAU, the Metropolitan AAU, refused to recognize the New York Association, and it barely survived. But by 1964 the association gained membership in the Met AAU, and some of the association people became Met AAU officials. That was the start of modest respectability.

(The New York Association didn't become the New York Road Runners Club officially until 1976, when I decided to streamline the name, but it was called that informally nearly from the start. We are still members of the RRCA, the original parent group, but in reality we have outgrown the RRCA and haven't much relationship with them, aside from the race insurance we get through them.)

But back when I got the idea for having a marathon in Central Park, I didn't know all these ins and outs. The association seemed to be just a paper organization, without even an office that I knew of, so to me the association and the Met AAU were one and the same. I called up the Met AAU and said I'd like to sponsor a marathon. They seemed uninterested. They said I should send them a letter in triplicate. I decided instead to make a presentation directly at one of their meetings.

I made my pitch. I told them I had some wealthy friends (exaggerating a little) who would help me sponsor a marathon in Central Park.

Everybody at the table was very negative about it: A) You can't get Central Park because the Parks Department won't give you permission. B) No one's going to want to run in Central Park because it's not safe. C) The Police Department won't cooperate. And so on.

I was angry. Here I thought I was proposing something to them that would be very exciting, and money wasn't even a factor. But they didn't even want to consider it.

So I walked out. Vince Chiappetta, who by then was president of the RRCA, followed me, and put a hand on my shoulder. He said, "You know what, Fred? Ignore them. *We'll* do it. You and me."

Vince was a biology teacher and a smoother talker than I was. After we discussed it a couple of times, we went to the Parks Department together, and I let him do the talking. Surprisingly, the Parks Department was not negative. I don't think they quite knew what we were talking about, but they gave us permission for the marathon.

Vince and I were codirectors of the race. Ted Corbitt, who would run in it (as would Vince and I), measured the course; an expert at that, he literally wrote the book on course measurement and worked with the precision that is still the standard today. We typed up entry blanks. Entry fee was one dollar.

But we didn't get any publicity. The Parks Department and others said they would put out the word, but nothing happened. The summer dragged on, and we had only a handful of entries. Finally, in September, about a week before the marathon, I walked into the newsroom of *The New York Times* and said I'd like to talk to somebody about the New York City Marathon. They had never heard of it. They sent me to some guy who asked me, "Who's running in it?" I said, Ted Corbitt, who was on the

Olympic marathon team at Helsinki in 1952 and was national champion in 1954. I mentioned some other stuff, but it was Corbitt's name that did it, and from then on I knew that names were the key to getting publicity for an event.

The Times ran a small story the next day, and we managed to get 126 entries.

Not surprisingly, my "wealthy friends" failed to materialize when it came time to put out some money. So I sponsored it by myself, as far as money was concerned. The day before the marathon, Vince and I went to Greenwich Village to buy a few cases of soda because we could get it three cents per can cheaper there. Vince knew somebody at Tavern-on-the-Green, the fancy restaurant in the park where the start and finish lines would be, and they donated a pile of sandwiches. For prizes I bought fifteen wristwatches for ten dollars each.

It wasn't much, but it was more than anybody else had done in New York before. Though we didn't even have a police patrol, we did have the New York City Bike Patrol, a volunteer safety unit, to help shepherd the runners.

And we had our marathon. It went off without a hitch. There were no crowds and no problems. It was won by Gary Muhrcke, a New York City fireman, in a time of 2:31:38. There were fifty-five finishers (two women started but did not finish). I did not see Muhrcke's victory because I was back in the pack. I finished forty-fifth in a time of 4:12:09.

When I came across the finish line, I was ecstatic, not because I finished, but because we did it! We put on a marathon and it worked!

I couldn't wait to do it again in 1971. I actually counted off the days on my calendar. I sponsored it again, and we more than doubled our field, with 246 starters and 164 finishers. Norm Higgins of Connecticut won and broke our record with a time of 2:22:54.

But the big news of 1971 was the women. Five started, four finished, and nineteen-year-old Beth Bonner, of New Jersey, became the first woman in the world to run a marathon officially in under three hours: 2:55:22. Right behind her was our own

Nina Kuscsik, in 2:56:04—we had the two fastest women marathoners in the world! Nina, a nurse, was a member of our club and one of the most important pioneers in women's running. Those days were the dawn of distance running for women.

Actually, women were not then permitted by the AAU to run officially in distance races with men. But there were no long-distance road races being put on for women either. There were those people—such as Olympic officials—who believed that women couldn't or shouldn't run long distances: They were too fragile. Their bodies were different. They were *women*.

In point of fact, there were so few women distance runners because there were so few opportunities. Clearly, women could and should run, and I figured their participation was not only fair and proper but would also attract attention for us.

I needed an angle, and one presented itself almost out of the blue.

The public relations company representing Johnson's Wax contacted me to say they wanted to sponsor a marathon for women and use it to promote a product called Crazy Legs, a shaving cream for women.

I said, "Are *you* crazy? There are only two women I know of in the entire state of New York who have ever even *run* a marathon."

Still, they wanted to sponsor a long-distance race for women. So I made a suggestion. Miniskirts were fashionable then. I suggested that we put on a shorter race—a 6-miler—and call it a minimarathon. They went for it.

Kathrine Switzer helped me produce it. Kathy was the first woman distance runner to attract widespread press attention. In 1967 she had entered the men-only Boston Marathon as "K. Switzer," with her long dark hair tucked under a cap and wearing a sweat suit. A few miles into the race, the marathon director recognized her as a woman and tried to knock her off the course. But her big boyfriend interceded and batted the man away, and Kathy went on to finish. (Now she is director of the Avon International Running Circuit, the largest program for women, producing races all over the world.)

The PR firm mailed out 35,000 letters to high schools and colleges all over the area, inviting women to enter. And I worked feverishly to promote it. I handed out leaflets and entry blanks everywhere I went, I taped flyers to light poles. Some people thought it was a joke. I didn't care what they thought, so long as we got a field of women runners and attracted some attention. Sometimes I embarrassed Kathy. Once we were at Max's Kansas City, a Lower East Side rock-music hangout, having dinner. In the middle of it I went around to all these spaced-out rocker-type girls and tried to get them to take entry blanks. Nothing embarrassed me. I even recruited six Playboy Bunnies to run—a great promotion!

Eventually, we managed to sign up seventy-eight women. The race was a huge success. (The Bunnies hopped along until they were out of sight of the crowd, then dropped out.) The minimarathon caught on instantly, spawned a host of women's races all over the place, and grew incredibly. The "L'eggs Mini Marathon," an annual 10-K (6.2 miles) race, drew a field of 6,500 women in 1983.

(Johnson's Wax discontinued their product when they were sued by former football great Elroy "Crazylegs" Hirsch for name infringement.)

In 1972 that was a big breakthrough. It also served to draw attention to the fact that women had been running our marathon. The Met AAU decreed that women could not start our marathon together with the men. The women's start would have to be ten minutes before the men, creating a separate race. We had six entrants that year. When the gun went off for the women's start, all six, led by Nina Kuscsik, sat down. They stayed right where they were for the full ten minutes, until the gun went off for the men's start, and they ran with the men.

After that the AAU, faced with a threatened lawsuit from the women, relented, and from then on women have been allowed to run with men in road races.

The year 1972 was notable for other reasons, too. It was the year I had a big fight with the leaders of our club. It was a turning point.

I had sponsored the marathon for two years, and it had worked. Now it was time to take another step, to make it really go. I decided that, now that we had established it, there was no reason why I should have to sink my own money into it anymore and lose it. I didn't think it had to be a money-losing proposition at all.

I invited the club leaders to my apartment to discuss a proposition. (In those days there were no offices. I did the marathon work on my kitchen table.) Maybe ten or twelve people. I set up food and drinks, and I made my proposal. It was pretty simple. I proposed that we produce a professional-looking entry blank—a two-color entry blank that would be attractive enough to take to Boston, for example, where I could promote our race at the Boston Marathon. And we should produce an official marathon program in a magazine format. We could sell ads for the program. All it would take is an investment up front by the club of three hundred dollars to print the entry blanks and commit the club to a marathon program.

They agreed it was a terrific idea. Then somebody raised the question: What if it loses money?

It was dumb to be concerned about such small potatoes. But I said, if it loses money, I'll subsidize it. I paid for the first year and the second year, and if I have to, I'll pay for it again. I knew it wouldn't lose money, but that wasn't the point. I explained that I wanted the club to get more involved, that sponsorship should not be a one-man operation. The club needed to make more of a commitment, and that meant a financial commitment up front, as well as a manpower commitment down the line. But in any case, I guaranteed that the club would not lose any money because I would back it up with my own.

With that promise they voted for it. Then, when they were about to leave, someone said, "Where's the check?" What check? I said. "We should have your check for printing the entry blank— three hundred dollars," he said.

"Wait a second," I said. "First, the club is going to pay for it.

And second, the money won't be lost because we'll sell ads in the program. And third, if the money doesn't come in, I've already said I'd cover the cost."

"But suppose we put up the money and you die tomorrow," he said.

I was furious. I yelled and screamed—I don't remember what I said. The dispute was frustrating and pointless—all I could do was rage.

But I do remember what I thought. When they left my apartment—leaving the matter up in the air—I thought: Here's a sport that's very viable, something so vibrant and exciting, with potential that is just incredible, yet it's in the hands of people who are afraid to put up three hundred dollars, which I have guaranteed, because I may die tomorrow.

I thought: There's only one way this will succeed. And that is if I never listen to them. I must completely ignore them. For the marathon to be a success the way I was starting to dream of it, they must be ignored, and I must do my own thing. My way.

I put together a program. On the cover it said, in red and black type:

Third Annual NEW YORK CITY MARATHON Official Program. Sunday, October 1, 1972, at 11 a.m., Central Park.

Sanctioned by: The Met. Assoc. of the Amateur Athletic Union of the U.S.

Sponsored by: Road Runners Club of America, New York Association.

With the cooperation of The Department of Recreation of the Parks, Recreation and Cultural Affairs Administration, City of New York.

The cover photo showed Gary Muhrcke winning the first New York City Marathon in 1970. There were twelve pages inside, including a page of photos from the 1971 marathon (one showed Erich Segal, author of *Love Story,* and me running side by side); the 1972–73 race schedule with what were now twenty club races which, for the first time, extended year-round; and the names, ages, and best previous times of every entrant (we showed 210, but we actually had 284 by race day).

I sold all the ads. Primarily I sold them to my textile company and all the other companies I had dealings with (so there were ads from Downen Zier Knits, Tucker Knits, Embe Knitting Mills, Atlas Knitting Mills, and so on).

I also sent out a letter to every single club member—more than two hundred—asking for help. I made them patrons for $5, sponsors for $10, benefactors for $20. I was very disappointed with the response, but we did get thirty-five patrons and eighteen sponsors.

As it turned out, I didn't sell enough ads and had to kick in a little of my own money to cover it, but the program went over very well and put some substance into our marathon. It was the forerunner of our official program today, which, as a special edition of our *New York Running News,* is a glossy, four-color magazine of about 150 pages.

When Frank Shorter won the gold medal at the Summer Olympics in Munich, there was suddenly a big surge of interest in marathons. The public at large had become aware of the marathon. For the first time I thought a running boom might be imminent. I wanted to capitalize on that right away.

General Motors had just opened up a big, classy building at the corner of Fifth Avenue and 59th Street, near the southeast corner of Central Park. And they had just come out with some kind of experimental pollution-free car. I had the bright idea that on the heels of all the publicity about Shorter we could get GM involved with our marathon. We wrote a letter to GM proposing that we have the start and/or the finish right in front of their new building and that we could use this new experimental car as our lead car—a car that wouldn't spew exhaust fumes in the faces of the lead runners. I thought it would be great publicity for GM. In exchange, I asked that GM sponsor the marathon for $2,000.

They rejected the proposal. They said they didn't have the budget for that kind of event.

General Motors, one of the largest corporations in America, didn't have $2,000 to invest in such a sensible promotion? Small thinking was everywhere.

I doubled my efforts. And despite the confrontations and frustrations, the 1972 marathon was our biggest and best yet, with 284 starters and 187 finishers. Even the women's sit-down strike at the start I considered a plus: It gave us a united front in efforts to include women; it was a significant part of the pressure that opened things up for them, and it gave us publicity.

Sheldon Karlin, a University of Maryland student, won in 2:27:52. Nina Kuscsik was the women's winner, officially in 3:08:41 (from which you subtract the ten minutes of sit-down strike for her actual time).

By 1973 the club had grown to eight hundred members. I was elected president, and we had our first big sponsorship breakthrough. Olympic Airways, of all things. Kathy Switzer introduced me to Nancy Tuckerman, who had been a secretary to Jacqueline Onassis and was now head of public relations for Olympic Airways, which Aristotle Onassis owned. Kathy urged me to get Nancy involved.

I took Nancy to see the Yonkers Marathon, in May, and she was captivated by the event. She got Olympic Airways to sponsor our 1973 marathon for $5,000, which was a lot of money to us in those days. Olympic would also take the winner to the Pan-Hellenic Marathon in Athens—a big promotional plus all around.

Kathy was my codirector for the marathon that year. Olympic Airways provided personnel at the water stations around the course during the race. We had 406 starters (the women's field doubled to 12) and 287 finishers. Tom Fleming, from New Jersey, set a record of 2:21:54. Nina Kuscsik was again the women's winner, in 2:57:07.

Meaning to capitalize on a bit of history, we had this marathon finish at Columbus Circle, just outside the southwest corner of the park. I understood that the very first marathon run in New York, in 1897, had been from Stamford, Connecticut, to Columbus Circle. (We finished there in 1974 and 1975, too. But then facts came to light that the finish in 1897 had not been at

Columbus Circle, but at Columbus Oval, in the Bronx. We reverted to having the finish within Central Park, where it was anyway more convenient and easier to control, and every finish since has been at Tavern-on-the-Green.)

We were extremely happy with the quality of the 1973 race, the ever-bigger field, the new record. And because of having sponsorship, not only were we able to pay our bills but we were able to rent a cafeteria for a sit-down dinner for all the runners.

In 1974 Olympic Airways upped its sponsorship to $8,000. We rented Heuer electronic timing equipment for the first time. One last-minute screw-up threatened disaster: It was pouring rain that day, and the Parks Department assumed the race would be canceled because of it. So parks personnel, on whom we depended for patrol and control and help with a thousand details, didn't show up. I went crazy trying to round up volunteers to help, and the race went off smoothly anyway. The lesson was forever learned by the Parks Department and everybody else— we run our races regardless of weather.

We had 527 entrants, including 26 women. We had new winners: Dr. Norbert Sander in 2:26:30 and my friend Kathy Switzer in 3:07:29. And we got a burst of national publicity. Kathy and Dr. Sander appeared on the *Today* show, and *People* magazine ran a story.

Then a setback: Onassis died in March 1975. Shortly thereafter, Olympic Airways withdrew its sponsorship. Having raised our sights because of Olympic's money, we were suddenly stripped. We begged all over the lot for help. We didn't get another sponsor, but 160 people sent in donations to defray costs. We lost quite a bit of money on the 1975 race. But fortunately we had momentum by then, and some status. We were able to get the AAU to sanction the marathon as the National AAU Women's Championship.

Ironically, it was the only year ever that we didn't have an increase of male entrants (490 against 501 the year before). But we still had a larger field overall, and appropriately that was because we had 44 female entrants, of whom 36 finished—an increase of 400 percent in female finishers. Kim Merritt, from the

University of Wisconsin, just twenty years old and in the early stages of what would be a splendid international running career, won our first national championship with a new women's record of 2:46:14. Tom Fleming lowered his men's record to 2:19:27.

And that year we got a new and important involvement from a city official—Manhattan Borough President Percy Sutton. Sutton was a savvy and ambitious politician with designs on becoming the city's first black mayor. George Spitz, a longtime participant and gadfly in marathon matters, had some connections with the borough president's office, and he urged me to invite Sutton to be the official starter of the race. I invited, Sutton accepted. Not only did he fire the starter's pistol, but he surprised me by staying around for the finish. He placed the laurel wreath on the head of Kim Merritt, and it immediately slid off—an incident that caught the attention of a *Daily News* photographer. His picture made the front page, our first page-one publicity.

Sutton's participation was more significant than we had realized. Little did we know that 1975 would be the last year for our marathon to be relatively small, and confined to Central Park. The next year would see our race break out and go city-wide, launching us onto the national and international marathon stage.

Percy Sutton never became mayor. But in 1976 he opened the gates for the New York City Marathon.

4

When I was a refugee kid roaming around Europe, fresh from Rumania, people would say, "Are you a bloodsucker?"—teasing me because I was from a province of Transylvania. I didn't know the significance of Count Dracula then. But I knew the significance of other scary things, like bombs and Nazis. War had caused my family to split up and flee. From an early age I was learning about living by your wits, always being on your toes, improvising.

I was born in 1932 in Arad, in western Rumania about ten miles from the Hungarian border, forty miles from Yugoslavia. I was the sixth of seven children—four older brothers, one older sister, and one younger sister. We were an orthodox Jewish family. There were about 10,000 Jews in the city of about 100,000.

My father was a produce merchant. He bought and packaged and shipped freight-car loads of fresh fruit and vegetables, and sometimes poultry, to Bucharest. We lived nicely in a typical stone house with a courtyard in back. People thought we were rich because we were one of the few families in town to have a telephone and a radio, but we weren't.

My father's business, at which my mother and older brothers also worked, was a pleasant kind of business, very colorful. Our city, largely industrial, was surrounded by half a dozen agricultural villages, each with its own ethnic quality, like enclaves, where they kept their own language and customs—Bulgarian, Hungarian, German, Rumanian, and Gypsy villages. Each village had its own specialty—the Bulgarian village was known for watermelons and canteloupe, the German for vegetables like cucumbers, radishes, green peppers, tomatoes. Another village specialized in peaches.

People from these villages would bring their produce to my father's warehouse, or he would go to the villages to crate produce on the spot. Except the Gypsy village. They were the most fearsome kind of Gypsies. We stayed away from them. My favorite thing to do was to go with my father to these villages. In the summer he would organize whole classes from school for outings to pick peaches. The kids would sing and have fun and eat all the peaches they could.

In these villages my father would know everybody, and part of the fun was being greeted by so many friendly people. It was very much an honor-system business. I saw very little bookkeeping going on.

In town the population was mostly Rumanian and Hungarian. We were Rumanian. At home we spoke Yiddish, on the street Rumanian and Hungarian. All of us spoke German, too, because our strongest business relationship was with the German community. We were a happy, close family. As a child, my thinking was that happiness was only if your whole family stayed together—even after everybody was married. I was not an athletic kid. I played a little soccer, because all kids there did, but I wasn't any good. My father was very strict about the importance of studies, with the Talmud as the base.

I was probably about ten when we started hearing rumors about Jews being mistreated by Nazis in various parts of Europe. But we didn't believe the rumors. The Germans that we knew wouldn't be capable of that. Then the refugees started arriving— from Hungary, Germany, Poland—to seek safety in my hometown. We learned about concentration camps.

And we began hearing even worse rumors about what was

happening to Jews. One time a German farm lady came to us very upset because she had received a letter from her son saying that he had a terrible job in Germany: As a soldier working in a concentration camp, his job was exterminating Jews. My father took the letter to Jewish community leaders, who thought the words were a mistake. "Exterminating" was a misspelling or something, because we still couldn't believe such a thing was going on.

Then the Nazis came to occupy our town. We knew by then that the first thing they did was send Jews to concentration camps. But the Rumanian government was not anti-Semitic and didn't bend so easily to Hitler's wishes. The prime minister contended that it would be a better idea to keep the Jews in Rumania, to help build the country's defenses against the Nazi foes, the Russians. It was just a ruse, of course, to keep the Jews from being sent to concentration camps. But it worked. They took all the Jewish men between the ages of eighteen and sixty away to a nearby work camp. There was no real work to do. They would take a big pile of earth and move it from one side of the road to the other and then back again.

My father and older brothers were sent there. We couldn't visit them, but they could receive packages. My mother even sent them white bread, which was against the law because bleached flour was scarce and expensive. She would use a little brown sugar to color the bread, make it appear dark. And they could come home on Jewish holidays. It wasn't pleasant, but it wasn't so awful either. It was better than other situations we had heard about from refugees.

Of course, they forced my father to give up his business. Jews were not allowed to own any businesses. What my father did was to give the business to one of his Gentile employees, who was a good friend. He was owner in name only. In reality he continued to run it for my father.

The war came closer. We began to hear explosions. A building near us was bombed, and people were killed. When cannon fire was very close to the city, the German troops began pulling out. They left in a hurry. The war was about over. My father and brothers came home. We were waiting to welcome the Russians as liberators. The town even built a huge gate to welcome the Russian troops as they came in.

But it didn't happen, not then. The Germans came back in with a vengeance. And Hungarian soldiers with them, as allies. Their tents took over all the backyards.

One morning there was a hubbub outside, and Hungarian soldiers rushed out of our backyard with their guns. When they returned a little while later, I heard one of them say, "It was a Jewish boy, but one-two-three I finished him off." One of my brothers was arrested when a German officer said that my brother had spit on his boots. When the officer came by our house, my mother walked over to him and put her hand on his shoulder and said gently, "Perhaps, officer, it was a mistake." The officer said, "Take your bloody Jewish hands off me."

By using our contacts with the local police, we got my brother released. But things were getting very serious. They ordered the Jews to wear yellow stars, which we hadn't had to do before. And by now we knew that was the first step to concentration camps. Sure enough, we were supposed to start wearing the yellow stars the following week, and then on the Friday of that week all Jews were to report to a military camp—an old abandoned barracks on the other side of the Mureşul River—standard Nazi procedure we had been warned about.

We knew we had to escape. We couldn't all go together. My father and oldest brother built a temporary hiding place in the house—put a big bookcase in front of the door to a large pantry. They would stay there. My two sisters went to hide in the house of some German friends. My mother, my other brothers, and I dressed as farmers and set out walking. We walked miles and miles to a Bulgarian village where we were known and began knocking on doors asking people to take us in. Everybody was sympathetic, but they were all too scared.

I was scared, too. It was getting dark and cold. Bombings and gunfire were all over the place. My knees were trembling. With every explosion they shook more. That is something that has stayed with me to this day: If something frightens me, my knees tremble.

Then we heard a small voice: "Madam Lebowitz!" It was a teenage girl calling softly from a window. "Madam Lebowitz, please come in!" It was somebody we knew, and she said she could hide us in an upstairs room, but she reminded us that her father was a drunk and hated Jews.

We hid in the room for two days. Sure enough, on the third night the father came home drunk. We heard him ranting downstairs. The next morning the girl told us we would have to leave—her father suspected something.

We left. The gunfire was worse than ever. Shells whistled by. We found ourselves walking right behind a front line, where German soldiers hunkered down with their rifles.

There was no place to go to escape the war. We decided to go back home and face whatever we had to face. That night the "owner" of my father's business hid us in the company basement. All night long there was yelling and screaming and shooting and bombing.

In the morning the friend knocked on the door and said, "Everything's over, the Russians are here."

There were dead soldiers and dead horses all over the place. Dead soldiers with their boots gone because the first thing the Russians did was take their boots. These were the first dead bodies I had ever seen. I remember thinking it wasn't such an awful sight because they looked very peaceful. They were very young; they looked hardly older than I was.

The Russian soldiers inspected the barracks where the Jews had been supposed to report under Nazi orders. They found that the rooms were equipped for pumping in gas. The gas was in place. That was a Friday, when the Russians came in, the same day we had been ordered to report to the barracks.

Only later did we learn the extent of the damage to our extended family. We were the only ones saved. All the rest—grandparents, uncles, aunts, cousins, who had been living in Hungary and Czechoslovakia—were exterminated.

At first, everything was friendly with the Russians. But then they began to impose their own order. They confiscated my father's business because no individual could own a business. It was clear we would not have freedom, and our town would not again be such a happy place. We started making plans to leave.

We were not allowed to leave. Since we couldn't go as a family, we would have to split up to sneak away. We would go our separate ways, eventually to meet up again, perhaps in the new state of Israel. In 1947 one of my brothers slipped out first. Then it was my turn.

A group of several hundred orphan kids had special permission to leave and go to Czechoslovakia. These were kids the Russians were glad to get rid of, so they didn't have to worry about caring for them. They were being taken out by a Zionist group. My family knew the leaders of this group, and we decided to take advantage of it. Another of my brothers and I mixed in with the group and got aboard the train.

When we came to the Hungarian border, guards counted the kids. They lined them up by fives for the count. My brother and I were younger and smaller than the others. We hid behind the taller kids. There was a certain amount of confusion and haste to get the train moving again, so they missed us. When we came to the Czech border, my brother and I hid in the baggage compartment. There was a man assigned to watch the baggage compartment, but for a small baksheesh—bribes were common in those places those days, and we knew all about it—from the money our parents gave us, he looked the other way.

We stayed in Marienbad for a while, a beautiful place. We studied at the free Hebrew school and did odd jobs to make ends meet. After a couple of years we started roaming around—Belgium, Holland, England.

You couldn't really go freely like that from one country to another. But things were pretty confused and open-ended, with the war just over. There were thousands of refugees all over the place, some kids like us without families, wandering from one city to another, one country to another. And since we were young, people didn't bother us much. It was a "flower child" existence in a way. Strangely, I liked that life-style. We became experts at train hopping, hiding in baggage cars, spreading a little baksheesh around judiciously.

During this time my father, who knew people along the Hungarian border, got involved with helping Jews escape from Rumania. He was caught, arrested, beaten up. Somehow, with money and political pull, he managed to get out of jail and escaped to Israel with the rest of the family.

I wasn't ready to go to Israel yet. It was challenging, fun in a way, to live by my wits when I was fifteen and sixteen years old. My brother was very studious. But I began to go in other directions. I got involved with smuggling.

First it was sugar. It was profitable to smuggle sugar from one country where it was cheaper to another country where it was more expensive. Eventually it was diamonds. I got hooked up with some business types who were smuggling diamonds from Ostend, Belgium, to Dover, England, where the price was higher. I was just a courier, working for a fee. I never even knew the value of what I was carrying. The diamonds were packaged in double prophylactics. For a fee the equivalent of about two hundred dollars a trip, I would hide the diamonds on myself where an ordinary search wouldn't discover them and take the shuttle boat to Dover, where I would give them over to the people on the other end of the business. I was a trustworthy courier, and I did this several times before I made a mistake. I had gotten so comfortable carrying out these missions that one time when I got to Dover I forgot myself and went to the bathroom, and the diamonds went down the drain. I never dared go back to Belgium.

I went on to Ireland, where I got lodging in a castle, in county Westmeath. It was an actual castle, with four towers and a moat and beautiful gardens. It housed a kind of international education center. Part of it was a Hebrew school, where I studied.

All this time I had attended school sporadically someplace, and always a Hebrew school, because my father had instilled in us so firmly the importance of education. I was never a good student. I was diligent, but I had to work twice as hard to keep up.

After some time in Ireland I became an Irish stateless citizen, with a passport. I decided I didn't want to go to Israel. I wanted to go to the United States.

In 1951 I managed to get a scholarship to a Talmudic academy in Brooklyn and was able to come to the States as a student. I was nineteen. It was a very serious school. But I was becoming a less serious student. Though I still believed that the Talmud was the basis for all knowledge, I felt it was too narrow and confining for the new world of life I was getting to know. I was becoming less orthodox. I had become used to adventure, and I wanted more.

To me, where I was in Brooklyn was not the United States of my dreams. It was an ethnic community more like Europe. I wanted to see the real America. When a new Talmudic school opened up in Kansas City, looking for adventurous students, that's where I went.

Middle America was okay, but school was not. I realized in Kansas City that I simply was not cut out to lead an academic life. One of my brothers had immigrated to Cleveland. I quit school and went to visit him. Once there, I decided to stay.

I wasn't allowed to work because I was here on a student visa. But that was easy enough to get around. I changed my name. Instead of Lebowitz, I went to the Social Security office and got a card under the name of Fred Lebow. I didn't have to show them anything, they didn't ask any questions, and I have been Fred Lebow ever since. When I got my U.S. citizenship ten years later, my legal name became Lebow (pronounced with the accent on the first syllable; but so many people have always put the accent on the second syllable, making it sound French, that I have given up correcting anybody).

In Cleveland I got a job as a salesman for a wholesale television distributor and made a good living. And I got involved with some theater people. I liked theater. Eventually I became part owner of an improvisational-comedy theater called Left-Handed Compliment, in the suburb of Cleveland Heights. Based on the Chicago group Second City, our nightclub became an instant success. I quit my job and devoted myself to it. I came to New York to audition actors, and we brought in four or five. I myself got on the

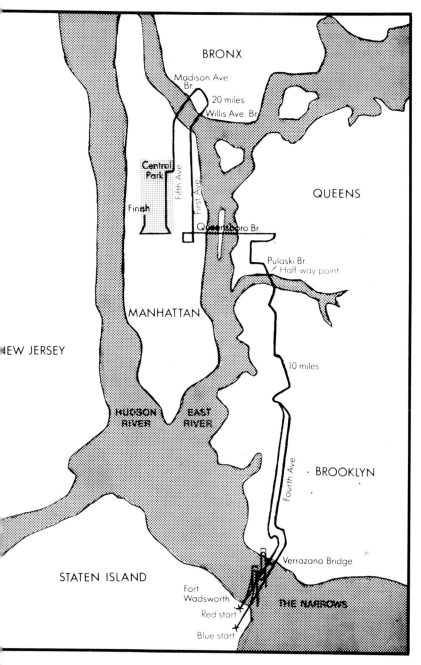

The New York City Marathon course—26 miles, 385 yards, cross five bridges, and through all five boroughs *(Madonna Daniel Woodley)*

Vincent Chiappetta,
co-meet director *(left)*
and Kurt Steiner at
the first New York
City Marathon awards
ceremony, September
13, 1970
(Walt Westerholm)

Gary Muhrcke crosses
the finish line in the
first New York City
Marathon, September
13, 1970.
(Walt Westerholm)

Kathy Switzer runs the 1974 marathon, which she went on to win. *(Paul J. Sutton/ Duomo)*

Nina Kuscsik crosses the finish line as the female winner of the 1972 New York City Marathon. *(Steven E. Sutton/Duomo)*

Running up the passageway over the FDR Drive is Micki Gorman, thirty-nine, the female winner of the 1976 New York City Marathon. *(Gale Constable/Duomo)*

Bill Rodgers wins the first five-borough marathon in 1976, the first of his four straight New York City victories. *(New York Daily News Photo)*

The start of the 1976 New York City Marathon at the
Verrazano Narrows Bridge *(Janeart Ltd.)*

Bill Rodgers *(right)* duels with B. J. Bjorkland on Manhattan's First Avenue just before Rodgers sprints away to win the 1977 Marathon. *(New York Daily News Photo)*

Runners pose with *(front row, from left)* Jack Rudin, Mayor Abraham Beame, Manhattan Borough President Percy Sutton, and Fred Lebow at a City Hall press conference prior to the 1976 New York City Marathon. *(Paul J. Sutton/Duomo)*

Allan Steinfeld runs the 5 Mile Race, sponsored by Shamrock Marathon, at Virginia Beach, 1980. *(TSC Graphics, Inc.)*

At New York City Hall, Fred Lebow watches as Mayor Ed Koch reaches into a giant running shoe to draw the names of the first lotte entrants for the 1980 marathon. *(© Lisa Osta)*

Joe Kleinerman processes New York City Marathon applications. *(© Lisa Osta)*

stage once, when one of the actors was ill. I was an instant disaster. Even though it was improvisational, there were still a few lines you had to know, which were keys to skits. I couldn't remember any of them.

The theater was good for about two years. We relied heavily on advertising and on reviews every month or two, when we changed the show. When the Cleveland newspapers went on strike, we went instantly broke. I decided to seek my fortune in New York.

I had never been what you might call a natty dresser. I paid very little attention to my clothes. Ironic, then, that I should drift into the garment business.

I met some people in the business, and it sounded interesting. Double-knits were very big at the time, in the early 1960s, and I got a job with one of the more successful double-knit companies in New York, Tucker Knits, on Broadway. We produced "knock-off" fabrics and garments—stuff that looked like top-of-the-line expensive wear, but wasn't—for women. It was a totally new challenge, and I loved it. Every waking hour I studied the textile business, from the chemical end of it all the way to the finished garment. I worked on machines, worked with chemists, worked with designers, became an expert. They even sent me to the Fashion Institute of Technology.

Eventually, I decided to go into business for myself. With a partner I bought a factory in Brooklyn to produce knock-off fabrics and called it Arowtex. At the same time, I developed a consulting business, serving other clothing manufacturers.

Knocking off is always a good business. The secret was, you took an expensive woman's garment—say a three-piece suit that sold at Bloomingdale's for three hundred dollars—and produced something that looked and felt like it but cost less than half as much. You did that by skimping everywhere. Instead of making the jacket twenty-nine inches long, we'd make it twenty-seven. We'd eliminate the lining. Instead of six buttonholes, we'd have five. Instead of three pockets, we'd have three fake pockets. Instead of using 100 percent wool, we'd use 70 percent polyester and 30 percent acrylic. Instead of using a union shop, we'd produce it in Chinatown. Before you know it, you've saved 80 percent of the total cost. Most of this was mail order, and in mail order the numbers get very big. If I really wanted to do it well, and not skimp on the style, I would go to Hong Kong or Taiwan to have it made, and save on labor and raw materials. The more I did it, the more clients I got. They would bring me an expensive garment and I would show them how to knock it off.

I was doing very well, making an income in the middle five figures and living in a $69-a-month apartment and spending next to nothing on anything else. I saved up—an old habit of mine, which allows me freedom to follow my nose and be adventurous.

All of a sudden, in the late sixties and early seventies, about the same time I got involved with running, polyester died. Overnight, the fabric got a bad name. I smelled the decline and sold my business. I didn't make any money from the sale, but I didn't lose any either.

I took a job with a Long Island fabric company called Jayme and traveled around the country for them as a troubleshooter, while continuing my consulting business on the side.

By the time 1976 came around, I was working full-time for Jayme, doing consulting work, and putting on the first five-borough marathon. I was getting more calls in my office about running than about clothing. I continued my consulting business on a diminishing basis for a couple of years, but I gave up my Jayme job, and about a month before the marathon, I became a full-time NYRRC president and marathon director.

The five-borough marathon was not just a good idea whose time had come. It was actually the result of a misunderstanding. And once it was understood, credit for the idea cannot be given to me, because I was opposed to it.

What happened was that during 1975, George Spitz, who had prevailed upon me to get Percy Sutton to start that year's race, got into conversations with Ted Corbitt about the notion of putting on some different, special kind of marathon. Corbitt had been thinking for some time about a special marathon that would involve city-wide participation. What Corbitt had in mind was creating teams from each of the five boroughs and having them compete for team championships in a city marathon, to which prominent national and international runners might also be invited as participants.

Somehow, Spitz assumed that Corbitt was suggesting a marathon that went through all five boroughs, and he thought it a terrific idea.

Soon after the 1975 marathon Spitz came to me with his perception of Corbitt's idea—a five-borough marathon. I was instantly opposed to it. It was already difficult enough to put on a marathon in Central Park.

Spitz said he would like to talk to Percy Sutton about it. I said, fine, go ahead and pursue it. I didn't think anything would come of that. You couldn't run a marathon totally through city streets. Even the Boston Marathon, the oldest and then the most prestigious in this country, ran most of its course through the countryside and small towns, from Hopkinton to Boston, and only the last few miles were in Boston itself. I put it out of my mind.

Next thing I knew, Spitz wanted to set up a meeting. He had talked to Sutton and wanted us all to sit down together and discuss this idea. I kept stalling him. I thought it was an exercise in futility. And I didn't want to be put in the position of arguing about it, saying negative things.

Finally I couldn't stall any longer, and we met at the house of David Blackstone, who was coach of the Central Park Track Club, of which I was a member, and his wife, Lynn, who was also very active in running. Sutton was there, with Spitz, and I brought Brian Crawford, who was then on our executive committee.

Sutton was enthusiastic about a five-borough marathon. And, of course, I wasn't. Sutton asked me why I was objecting. I repeated the objections I had made to Spitz, about having enough trouble already with the marathon we had; that we'd never get all the permissions necessary—police protection, cooperation of all the other city departments likely to be needed, and so on. And above all, I said, it would cost us $20,000. Not only that, but the one sponsor we did have for two years, Olympic Airways, had dropped out, and we had lost money on the 1975 race.

I doubted it would cost as much as $20,000. I just tossed out that figure because it was high and I figured that would put an end to it.

Sutton listened to me, very cool. When I was finished, he said, "If I can get you the money, and get you the proper police protection and all, would you still object to it?"

Of course not, I said. What could I say? He was the borough president, an important and respected man, and I didn't want to offend him by saying that it would never happen.

A few days later he called to say he had a sponsor for $25,000 and the full support of Mayor Abe Beame, with full police protection guaranteed. It would be part of the celebration of the bicentennial year in New York.

My first thought was: What am I going to do with the extra $5,000? Because at the time even $20,000 seemed high to me.

My second thought was: I have a full-time job and a part-time consultancy business, and now we have to put on this five-borough marathon. How will we do it? Who's going to help? Where will it go? Who, what, where, when, why?

But then: We've got the city behind us, we've got a sponsor, we can go for it, in the bicentennial year. What an opportunity!

The sponsor was the family of Samuel Rudin, who had died earlier in the year. Founder of the Rudin Management Company, a big real-estate firm, and an active philanthropist, Samuel Rudin had been a long-distance runner fifty years ago. His sons, Jack and Lewis, would sponsor the marathon in memory of their father. They were big boosters of New York and staunch supporters of Percy Sutton.

We had several meetings at Sutton's office to discuss all the aspects of plans—technical, legal, logistical, financial. He put his staff at our disposal, and they were incredibly helpful, opening all the doors we couldn't have opened so quickly on our own with various city departments, such as police, fire, bridges, parks, highways. Even the entry blank was eventually printed by Sutton's office as an off-hours favor to us.

My kitchen table was no longer adequate work space, and we managed to get some room at the West Side YMCA through the efforts of Bob Glover, who was then fitness director there (he has since become director of educational programs for our club, as well as a running coach, author of running boks, and head of his own fitness-consulting firm).

In December, 1975 some key members of the club and I—Ted Corbitt, Joe Kleinerman, Kurt Steiner, Harry Murphy, Paul Milvy—set to work trying to figure out a course. We knew it would end in Manhattan and should start in Staten Island, and that it had to include Brooklyn, Queens, and the Bronx. Beyond that, the only certainty was that the course had to be precisely 26 miles 385 yards. We didn't even know how many runners the course would have to accommodate. If we were lucky, we might get a thousand or so, which would double the previous year's field.

From the Verrazano-Narrows Bridge, connecting Staten Island with Brooklyn, we surveyed all kinds of routes, measuring them with car odometers, assessing traffic patterns and road conditions. I wasn't looking for where the crowds would be or where the most interesting neighborhoods were. The idea was to eliminate problems. I anticipated that traffic control would be the number-one problem. I wanted a course that would cause the least traffic disruption, the least inconvenience to the city.

First of all, there was the question of bridges. The Verrazano Bridge would get us from Staten Island to Brooklyn. Then there were a whole bunch of alternatives to get us from there to the Bronx and Manhattan. First we thought of the Triborough Bridge linking Queens with both the Bronx and Manhattan. But tying up traffic on that busy bridge seemed unreasonable. So we would have to go into Manhattan somehow and then into the Bronx via any one of several bridges, then back into Manhattan. We considered the Queensboro Bridge from Queens to Manhattan, and the Brooklyn Bridge from Brooklyn to Manhattan. I even thought the Brooklyn-Battery Tunnel was a possibility.

Finally we decided on a route. We would start at the Staten Island end of the Verrazano-Narrows Bridge, where the Army's adjacent Fort Wadsworth could serve as the staging area; come up through lower Brooklyn and hug the old Brooklyn Navy Yard, where there were not many cross streets and not much traffic. At about the thirteen-mile mark we would enter Queens, and at fifteen miles would cross the Queensboro Bridge into Manhattan. Then we would go north, right along the river, using the sidewalk bordering the East River Drive. We would cross into the Bronx via the sidewalk of the Willis Avenue Bridge and continue just a few yards to the twenty-mile mark, where we would make a U-turn around a light pole and return back across the bridge to Manhattan. We would head south on First Avenue, cross at 106th Street to Fifth Avenue, and down Fifth to 102nd Street, where we would enter Central Park. The final three miles would be down the Central Park East Drive, around the bottom of the park, and up the West Drive to the finish at Tavern-on-the-Green.

In all, we would have to close about 220 street intersections and use four bridges. We would need more than four hundred policemen assigned to coordinate traffic control. I heard that the first reaction of the Police Department was: No way! Impossible to block all those intersections and disrupt traffic and control everything without inordinate problems, expense, and risk. But since the city insisted, the P.D. went along with it (and quickly became enthusiastic supporters of the marathon). It was planned that in April a representative from Sutton's office would go to Boston to observe traffic-control procedures at that marathon.

Corbitt and others repeatedly ran portions of the course and prepared detailed maps of potential problem areas. The course was measured several times by people riding specially calibrated bicycles following procedures developed by Corbitt.

We fixed a date, considering holidays and the dates of other marathons so as not to conflict: Sunday, October 24.

There was endless stuff to organize: processing of applications, volunteers (we would need about 450), ham-radio operators to give us communication links from start to finish, recruitment of elite runners, timing and scoring, press coverage. We had to design and produce T-shirts for the runners, create an official program, and arrange for such logistics as buses to carry the runners from Manhattan to Fort Wadsworth, pre-race supervision of the runners at Fort Wadsworth, and care for the runners after the finish, as well as accommodations for the awards ceremony.

One of the primary keys to making the race work over such a long route was (and is) radio communications. We met with the major ham-radio group in the area—the Tri-State Amateur Repeater Council—and made our pitch. Steve Mendelsohn, head of the group, agreed to join us and would provide twenty-five hams to be spaced along the route.

For the first few months we didn't put out any publicity, and nothing was in the papers. In early summer I called a press conference outdoors near the finish line to announce the spectacular, new, five-borough New York City Marathon. Percy Sutton was there with me. Not one member of the press showed up. Nobody. I had called it for midafternon, which I learned was never a good time for the press. But beyond that, nobody knew what this was all about. I might as well have been announcing that we were going to throw Frisbees on the Central Park lawn. By 1983 we would give out more than 2,000 press credentials. But at that time in 1976 I was shaken by the lack of interest. We would have to stir things up somehow. We needed names. That's when I decided to go after Frank Shorter and Bill Rodgers.

We also needed some foreign runners, to give the race an added, classy dimension. I didn't have any international contacts, except one, the fine English runner Chris Stewart. He was a good person to start with, because I had had something to do with his becoming a marathoner.

Back in 1973 Stewart had called me. I had never met him, but I knew his reputation as a star 10-K racer. He said he was in New York and that Kathy Switzer had recommended me as the man who could fix him up with a date for the evening. I said I would fix him up with a friend of mine if he would run a race for us. We had a 5-miler coming up. He ran our race, won, and set a course record.

A few weeks later he called again about finding a date. We had a 15-K race in the offing. He balked at the deal—it was longer than his normal competitive range. But later he called back and said, okay, if I had another attractive friend. He ran, won, and set our course record for the distance.

The next time he called, we had a 20-K race scheduled for the following day. Now the terms really upset him. He got angry. "You take me for a bloody *marathoner?*" he fumed. I said, "Have I ever got a girl for you!" This time I really went out of my way and produced a friend who was a gorgeous model from the Garment District. The next morning we had the race all ready to go, and he was nowhere in sight. I even delayed the start, hoping he would show up. At last he did. He stepped out of a taxi wearing a blazer and looking glassy-eyed. He changed clothes quickly. He ran, won, set a course record.

A couple of months later I got a call from the director of the Long Island Marathon, Paul Fetscher, who said that he noticed we had got Chris Stewart to run some of our longer distances and that he needed a name runner for his race. "How can I get Chris to run our marathon?" he asked. I said, "Are you crazy? I had to move heaven and earth just to get him to run our 20-K; a marathon is more than twice as long." He asked if there was a way to entice Stewart to make a show just for publicity's sake. I said, "I'll give you one clue: He loves women."

The next thing I knew, Chris Stewart was going to run the Long Island Marathon. I went out for the race. It was cold, snowing a little. He was standing at the starting line, shivering. "I'm just here to help with publicity," he said. "I'll just run part of the race." He ran, won, and set a record for that course.

I didn't hear anything from him for another year. Then I got a postcard from Fukuoka, Japan. He had just run the Fukuoka Marathon with a terrific time, 2:14. On the postcard, he had written: "Thank you."

So to help us assemble an international field for 1976, the first call I made was to Stewart. He agreed to come and gave me some other contacts. We got the British runners Ian Thompson and Ron Hill and Italy's Franco Fava (later director of the Rome Marathon). A good start.

As time went on, we quickly used up the $25,000 from our initial sponsor. It just went. I had reckoned it would be more than enough, and now I had to find more in a hurry.

I sent a proposal to Citibank, asking them to become a major sponsor for $10,000. The officer at Citibank didn't even send me a letter. He just scribbled on the face of the proposal something to the effect that they weren't interested and sent it back.

A runner and golf pro named Richard Metz, author of books on golf, had some connections with Manufacturers Hanover Trust Company and told me that the bank wanted to be a supporter of the marathon. I told him, no, the name is too long, it wouldn't fit anywhere—as opposed to a short, nifty name like Citibank. Well, he said, you might be able to pick up a couple thousand dollars from Manufacturers Hanover.

So I went to see Charles McCabe, a vice-president. He didn't know much about running, and less about the marathon. But he knew the value of promotion. I asked him for $10,000. He said he would give me $5,000 if the bank could have its name on the running numbers. For $5,000 the bank's name was short enough. Later on, when we wanted to have the award ceremony at Avery Fisher Hall in Lincoln Center, where the rental fee was $3,500, Charlie gave me that, too. (After MHT got all the publicity, Citibank put on some small runs in Central Park, and spent more than $100,000.)

Along the way we also picked up Finnair, which gave us $5,000 and provided the T-shirts. We also got $5,000 from *New Times* magazine, which was published by my friend George Hirsch. Hirsch, himself a marathoner, helped us further by printing a four-page marathon supplement in *New Times*. (The following year Hirsch produced the official program, and from that he launched *The Runner*, now one of the best and biggest magazines on the sport.)

Not all was roses, though. We would end up taking in about $45,000 and spending about $65,000, including some of my own money. Meanwhile, there were a million details to iron out, and I was by no means sure that we could pull everything together.

I had set up a Marathon Committee to coordinate everything, but it wasn't really functioning effectively. That was my fault. Delegating was not my style; I didn't know how to delegate. I didn't trust anybody to get things done. I was used to relying only on myself. So for a long time I tried to coordinate everything myself. The only substantial full-time help I had was Joe Kleinerman and Lynn Blackstone, who took several weeks off from her job with the Rockefeller Foundation.

I was particularly alarmed by the apprehensions of Gary Muhrcke, the winner of our first marathon in 1970 and subsequently a club officer. Gary had just started a business selling running shoes. He did his business, called Super Shoe on Tour, out of a van he brought to our races. On a Saturday morning a couple of months before the marathon he had his van at Central Park, and he was very worried about our plans to run the marathon through the city. He said, "Fred, you're flirting with disaster. It's a jungle out there. Running through rough neighborhoods like Bedford-Stuyvesant in Brooklyn, East Harlem in Manhattan—it's crazy."

Not only was Muhrcke very important to us, he was also a fireman, so he knew the city well. I pretended that I was sure of myself, knew what I was doing, and that everybody would be secure. But in point of fact, Gary scared me.

The next time I called a press conference, September 16, I had Frank Shorter, who had just won the Olympic silver medal in Montreal (having taken the gold in Munich in 1972). We flew him in for it. We got Mayor Beame and four borough presidents. And we got the press. We had Shorter run a few short sprints against Percy Sutton and the other chiefs, with Mayor Beame firing the starter's pistol—a bit of fun for the photographers.

We still didn't know how many runners we would get. But we now knew we would get a lot, and the question was: How many could we handle? Entries went past 1,000, past 1,500. They were pouring in faster all the time.

Allan Steinfeld joined the operation—I didn't even know about it. Paul Milvy, who was doing course measurement and seeing to other technical matters, was a biophysicist who had known Allan as a student seven years earlier, when Allan was also on the track team at City College of New York. Paul brought Allan in to serve as a chief timer. Allan brought in his girlfriend, Alice Schneider, who was working as a compositor on phototypesetting equipment. For us she would do data entry, for scoring, on a small IBM computer that was made available to us. (At first a volunteer, Alice would, through the years, teach herself computer programming and eventually would develop and manage the sophisticated computer operations we have today.) As important as they both were, their work was in an area I didn't poke my nose into, and I didn't meet either of them until after the marathon.

But that first computer operation, small as it was, suddenly became part of a big problem. It was a case of lost love fouling up our data bank.

The man who had put together the computer program for data entry from marathon-entry forms had been living with a woman and working with the forms in her apartment. They had a fight, and she kicked him out. About two hundred entry forms were in the apartment, and she wouldn't let him back in to get them.

We were getting frantic. Finally I called her. At first I tried to reason with her. I said, "Okay, so your boyfriend made you angry, or mistreated you, or whatever. But why should you punish the New York City Marathon because of that? Those entry blanks include entries from elite runners, some of the best in the world. You don't want to punish those fine athletes, do you?"

She was unmoved. So then I begged her: "Please have mercy on those athletes." I even pretended to cry. "Do you want to spend your whole life thinking that you've done something wrong like this?" She still didn't care.

We couldn't get the entries back. Ultimately, on marathon morning, just a couple of hours before the race, we had to set up a table at Fort Wadsworth for those two hundred runners to reenter the race. It was raining, so the entire field was crowded into the gym, and in the crush of all that and all the incredibly crazy last hours before the race, two hundred runners had to stand there filling out entire new entry forms.

That debacle is the reason we now spend several thousand dollars each year to have duplicate entry forms.

Two weeks before the marathon I saw to the painting of our first long blue line—now a tradition, covered every year since by the press—marking the entire course. We have a blue line on the road because once, running a marathon, I got lost.

In my first year of running marathons, when I ran thirteen, one of the last I ran was in Atlanta. There were only fifty to sixty entrants, so most of the way we were very spread out. To stay on the course, we relied on signs they had posted or on course marshals. About halfway through I was running alone and I came to a "T" intersection. There was no sign and no marshal. Whenever I don't know which way to go, whether I'm in a car or on foot, I will always take the turn to the right. So I turned right and continued running. For about half an hour I ran on. I didn't see any runners or any water stations. I started asking people along the way: Nobody knew anything about the marathon. So I gave up. I retraced my route and went all the way back to the start. An official told me there was supposed to be a sign at that intersection; someone must have knocked it down.

I knew right then that one requirement for a good marathon is that there be signs of some sort painted on the course, right on the road under your feet.

So that's why, in 1976 in New York City, we had to have a blue line. Actually it's long blue dashes, except for solid lines where the course turns. We have to do the work in the middle of the night, when there's least traffic. The Highways Department provides us with one of the trucks they use for street-lane marking, with a big paint drum on the back and a nozzle that sprays down on the road. We use a special paint, our own color called "Marathon Blue," which dries in a few seconds. The same

Highway Department guy, Sal Vitale, has been in charge of it ever since 1976.

That first year some of the route was on sidewalks. Those sections had to be done with a hand truck—something like what they use to put down foul lines on a baseball diamond or yard-line markers on a football field. There was this old guy who had to use the hand-pushed vehicle. And he didn't like it at all. He didn't like working in the middle of the night, he couldn't understand why we were doing it. Every ten yards he'd complain: Why do runners need a line? If they need directions, why not just little arrows once in a while? Do they actually have to *step* on the line? Can't they just follow a damn *map*?

I did everything possible to pacify him, keep him moving. But all the way up alongside the East River Drive, up the pedestrian ramps, down the pedestrian ramps, every ten yards he stopped to bitch and complain. Now the blue line takes us three or four hours on two consecutive nights. That first year, though, it took us a week of nights, or close to it.

By now things were so frantic with last-minute details that the office at the West Side YMCA was in chaos. Papers were spread all over the place, people were running in and out. Joe Kleinerman, who was registrar, took to sleeping on the floor by the telephone because it was ringing all hours with people asking questions. It was so busy that the club forgot to hold elections (so I continued as president without getting a vote).

We finally had to impose a cutoff date on entries so we could process them all, and it looked like we would have 2,100 runners from thirty-five states and twelve foreign countries—Japan, Finland, the Netherlands, Italy, Poland, West Germany, Norway, Ireland, England, Canada, the Philippines, and even Swaziland. In addition to the elite runners, we had some notables from other fields: Newark Mayor Kenneth Gibson; Jacques D'Amboise, of the New York City Ballet; and the oldest in the field, actor Robert Earl Jones, seventy-one, father of actor James Earl Jones. Ted Corbitt would run, at fifty-six. And we had former winners Tom Fleming, Norb Sander, Sheldon Karlin, and even Gary

Muhrcke—despite his misgivings. We had nearly one hundred women in the field from across the country, including Californian Miki Gorman, the tiny forty-one-year-old housewife and mother who had emigrated from Japan in 1964 and became the subject of a movie because of her running. Most of the women, though, came from the New York City area, including former winner Nina Kuscsik. But fully half the entrants were first-time marathoners.

For the first time ever we had to reject entries; about five hundred came in too late.

I could only pray that everything was being seen to and thought of.

Friday night, nine days before the marathon, I had a nightmare. In the nightmare New York was suffering from an awful drought, and there was no water available along the course for our two thousand runners. I took the lead car and rammed it into a fire hydrant, knocking it over so water would come out. I rammed the car into hydrant after hydrant along the course, blasting them open so our parched runners could get water to drink, until finally the front wheel of the car came off.

I woke up Saturday morning in a sweat. It was not just a nightmare, it was a message. I had managed to get people to man all the water stations in Manhattan but had forgotten about Brooklyn and Queens. It was one of those failures of mine to delegate, trying to do it myself, and that critical detail had simply slipped by. Runners could not survive without water on the first fifteen miles of the course; the entire marathon could become a disaster because of that one omission. And now I didn't know if there was time enough left to arrange for it.

I took our membership list and the map of the course, and Joe Kleinerman, who had worked for the Post Office for thirty-five years, provided me with the P.O.'s map of zip-code zones for correlation, and I started phoning.

I began with the Bay Ridge section of Brooklyn, the first area the runners would pass through after coming off the Verrazano Bridge. I got lucky. The first member I called said he could handle a water station and would get friends to help. My luck continued. I called maybe thirty areas, and virtually everyone I called was home to answer and was willing to help.

I thought: This is unreal! Why were people home for me?

I set up a meeting for the following Wednesday evening, for the people to pick up water cups and so on and get instructions. I prayed they would show up for the meeting. My luck held. All but one of the people I called showed up. I couldn't believe the cooperation. It was one of the moments you cherish for a long time, a marvelous omen for the race.

Frank Shorter arrived a couple of days before the marathon. I took him up in a helicopter for a bird's-eye tour of the course. When I looked down, I saw only places where things could go wrong. They could go wrong every place. Would the intersections be blocked off adequately? Or would some runner be hit by a car? Would the drawbridges we had to cross stay shut? Or would the Bridge and Tunnel Authority forget to tell some bridge operator, who would open a bridge and stop the marathon dead in its tracks? Would there be a fire in a building along the route, closing the street? Would people man the water stations? Would the timing clocks work at the finish line? Disaster lurked everywhere below.

Neither of us had been up in a helicopter before. I was in awe of Shorter. He was the first Olympic gold medal winner I had ever met. I couldn't even talk. We were both scared to death.

On Saturday, the day before the marathon, I went out for a walk on the Verrazano Bridge and discovered the expansion joints, which I hadn't noticed before. Big fingers of steel with spaces between them wide enough to trap a foot. The joints had to be covered. The Bridge Authority had nothing to cover them. I sent a volunteer to a Staten Island lumberyard to buy big sheets of half-inch plywood. The yard wouldn't accept a check. I had no cash. I went around the West Side YMCA gathering cash from anybody that had some. By late afternoon we had the plywood taped down over the expansion joints. I could only pray the plywood would work. If it didn't, we could have a disastrous pileup and injuries before the runners had gone one mile.

5

With more than two thousand entries we had suddenly become the world's largest marathon. Nobody before had ever had to manage the complexity of such a field of runners over that distance anywhere, and we were doing it all within a major city. A challenge unimaginable to me just a year before. Gary Muhrcke's ominous warning—we were flirting with disaster—rang in my ears.

I paced until 4 A.M., then I went to Fort Wadsworth, our staging area just off the foot of the bridge in Staten Island. It was about 40 degrees and drizzling rain. The sprawling grounds of the army base were dark and forbidding. In later years we would have huge tents on the grounds, and the Red Cross would be there with rolls and coffee and hot chocolate. But this first year there was none of that. I went into the gym, where at least it was light and dry. That was where the runners would gather for last-minute registration.

At 6 A.M. the buses began arriving with runners. The buses were on time! Before I knew it, the place was alive with athletes milling around inside the gym and out, stretching, taping ankles and knees, rubbing on liniment and Vaseline, wandering off into the woods to relieve themselves, babbling about their physical and mental condition, the weather, the course, the distance. We shouted instructions about where to deposit their baggage, which would be delivered back to the finish line for them, advisories about water stations, when to do what and where, but little could be heard above the din.

Ten minutes before the 10:30 start, we managed to get everybody up to the toll plaza on the bridge. We struggled to arrange the elite runners up at the front of the pack by themselves, where they could get a clear start, but it was impossible, all sorts of slower runners mixed in.

The police vanguard of motorcycles and cars was ready to roll. The small group of press people scrambled for places in the back of a pickup truck. I jumped into the van with which I would lead the race, beside Steve Mendelsohn with his walkie-talkie. The driver gunned the engine. Percy Sutton fired the starter's pistol. There was a roar from the mass of runners. We were off.

The first mile is uphill to the center of the bridge high over the Narrows. Behind us, the Finnish runner Pekka Paivarinta burst into the lead ahead of the pack. The plywood over the expansion joints worked!

Coming down off the bridge, I focused my attention ahead, preoccupied not with the race behind me, but with potential problems in front. Once the race started, the runners were on their own; my job was to make sure the course was ready for them.

The mileage markers were up! "3 Miles," "4 Miles." Some were taped to trees or lampposts, some were being held by volunteers.

There was a water station, people ready to hand out cups!

It was working!

At eight miles Paivarinta was almost a minute ahead of the lead pack—Rodgers, Shorter, Stewart, Fleming, Thompson. At that rate he was on a world-record pace. But it was too torrid for him to hold. Rodgers and Stewart, then Shorter, caught him.

I shot ahead to the Pulaski Bridge, which spans Newtown Creek between Brooklyn and Queens at the halfway point.

The barricades were set up wrong! The cops had set up the barricades so as to direct the runners across on the roadway instead of the walkway the course called for!

We screeched to a halt and I jumped out yelling at the police officer by the barricades. I started wrestling with the barricades while he tried to keep me away. I screamed obscenities and pushed him. He got angry and started hollering about arresting me. Somehow I got the barricades in position just before Mendelsohn rescued me from the law and yanked me back into the van.

At the middle of the bridge I ordered the van to stop again. I wanted to sit right there. It was a drawbridge, and on the slight chance that somebody might open it, at least they wouldn't open it with me sitting on top of it.

When the runners reached the foot of that bridge, I shot on to the Queensboro Bridge, to make sure no traffic blocked the roadway for our lead vehicles and nothing blocked the walkway the runners would use. Rodgers, swinging his white gloves, pulled away from Shorter and Stewart on the bridge.

Then up the East Side Drive in Manhattan, where the runners would use the sidewalk. We passed Dick Traum, a special hero of mine, who ran with an artificial leg. He had started the race alone on the Verrazano Bridge at 7 A.M., and here he was, looking strong. It would take him seven hours to finish. Seeing him provided a moment of inspiration.

A couple of miles up, the walkway veered off and was out of sight of the van. I moved on ahead to where the runners would reappear.

They didn't come! Thirty seconds seemed like thirty minutes, and I was terrified that they had turned off someplace. Maybe the rain had washed away parts of the blue line, or maybe there was a blockage of the course. I was in a panic, ready to jump out and run back along the walkway to find them, when suddenly Rodgers appeared, then Shorter and Stewart.

At the Willis Avenue Bridge I waited on the Manhattan side while Rodgers looped up onto the bridge heading into the Bronx. The runners were supposed to cross the short bridge, make a U-turn around a light pole on the Bronx side, and come right back.

What if they didn't make the U-turn! What if the course

marshal assigned there to make sure they turned didn't show up, and Rodgers continued straight ahead!

I had visions of the entire field following Rodgers like lemmings deep into the Bronx with no way to retrieve them. But once again, here came Rodgers, right on course. And behind him, Shorter, who had taken over second place by himself.

We wound our way down First Avenue, over to Fifth, down Fifth to the park. The intersections were pretty well blocked off. Occasionally a car would sneak through. Bicycles got in the way here and there. People didn't respect the marathon yet.

Our vehicles stayed just ahead of Rodgers all the way through the park. I didn't want him out of my sight again.

The finish line was a mess. The crowds were pressing in. The vehicles stopped, forcing Rodgers to go around them to finish. Then the press swarmed all over him. Shorter finished, then Stewart, both similarly swept up in the melee.

I was still desperately anxious about the rest of the field. Success would come from the average runners. Maybe they hated the race, maybe it was awful running through the city, stumbling over potholes and negotiating rain-slicked bridges and pedestrian ramps along the East River.

As the main part of the field started to cross the line, their faces showed nothing but exhaustion and pain, and they were engulfed by the crowd. I searched the faces. Finally there was one I knew, a guy who had run marathons all over the place.

I ran over to him. He embraced me and said, "Fred, it was fabulous! Fantastic! The best ever!"

It was a success!

Miki Gorman, the tiny Californian, came across the line, the women's winner, and fourteen minutes later the second woman, Doris Brown Heritage, from Seattle, Washington.

Pleasure, relief, and satisfaction swept over me all at once. The rest of the 1,549 finishers, including 63 women, came by in a blur.

The winners were crowned by laurel wreaths handmade by Gary Muhrcke's wife, Jane (a tradition carried on since; she gathers the laurel in the woods near their Long Island home). More than a thousand people celebrated the winners at the awards ceremony in Avery Fisher Hall. I basked in the sweet success while fifty trophies were handed out to overall winners, to age-group winners, to winning teams.

In the glow of the aftermath there was a marvelous outpouring of congratulations from the runners, the public, the city, from across the country, and even from foreign countries. *The New York Times* estimated that 500,000 spectators had watched along the course.

Mayor Beame proclaimed January 12, 1977, Fred Lebow Day, and we were feted at a reception at Gracie Mansion, with a bunch of city officials and other dignitaries.

On sober reflection I began to think that the 1976 marathon was the worst organized I had ever seen. The staging area at Fort Wadsworth and the start on the bridge were disorganized; for too much of the race I was in the dark about what was going on; the finish line was inefficient and disorderly. We had been lucky the race worked as well as it did, but I couldn't continue to trust to luck. We needed more volunteers; we needed a bigger communications system over the course; we needed more elaborate procedures to control the crowds at the finish and score the runners.

Allan Steinfeld quickly became a crucial part of the organization. We were in crying need of his technical abilities. He set about creating systems for us. He organized a technical committee to begin exploring solutions to the problems of handling these huge new fields of runners.

The first big technical breakthrough came at the mini-marathon in June, then sponsored by Bonne Bell, the cosmetics firm. Like the 1976 marathon, the mini would have two thousand runners. Unlike the marathon, those two thousand would be running only six miles, so the field would be much more condensed when it came to the finish line. Having two thousand in the mini was like having ten thousand in a marathon; at the peak, runners would cross the finish line at a rate of about one hundred per minute—too fast to allow accurate timing and scoring by the standard one-by-one method without creating a massive backup.

Since we couldn't decrease the rate of finishers, something had to be done to increase the capacity at the finish line.

Allan and his committee began devising the rudiments of the system we now have—which included a radical redesign of the finish line itself and the addition of computers (housed in a construction-type trailer) for data-entry scoring.

The finish line would be divided into three parts, creating, in fact, three finish lines at once under a single finish-line banner. Beyond each finish line was a series of four single-file chutes. Each finish line and its series of chutes operated independently with timing and scoring, so we tripled the capacity.

People handling long ropes that extended seventy-five yards in front of the finish lines would create lanes that divided the pack of runners into three fairly equal numbers and channeled them into each of the three finish lines; once past each finish line, the runners would be directed into the first chute until it was filled, then to the second, third, and fourth.

At the end of each chute were teams of two recorders, one who read off each runner's number, the other who wrote down each number in order. The finishing order was kept intact, even with several chutes being filled and emptied at once, because the chutes were designated alphabetically. After the first chute was filled and scored, a messenger would take the list of running numbers headed by the letter "A" and hurry it back to the data-entry trailer for entry into the computer; then would come a messenger with the "B" list, and so on through the alphabet. The chutes were filled and emptied in continuous rotation, and even if a chute filled later than but emptied before another, the order was kept proper because the prior letter would be entered first. We could keep processing all chutes simultaneously.

That meant that we had the order of finish by runner's numbers. A second operation did the timing.

Straddling each of the three finish lines were timers with

hand-held electronic stopwatches wired by umbilical cords to computers in the data-entry trailer. They were not concerned with numbers on the runners' bibs, just with bodies crossing the lines. As each body crossed the line, the timer would click his watch, and each click registered with the computer an exact time to the hundredth of a second.

So now, for each finish line we had a list of runners' numbers in order of finish, and we had a list of times in the computer. When these two lists were matched up, the times and the runners' numbers were correlated—each runner was matched up with an exact corresponding time. Then these results from the three finish-line systems were merged by the computer to produce the overall result.

Thus, if you had one hundred runners finishing per minute, each finish line had to process only about thirty-three. We could time and score all one hundred accurately without any backup at the finish line. A small version of this worked beautifully for the two thousand in the minimarathon.

So we would use it for the marathon. We had figured on three thousand entries. By August, two months before the marathon, we had five thousand, and were forced to close entries. We had to reject two thousand more that came in later.

The response of the relatively small crowds at the 1976 marathon had been so enthusiastic that the city wanted the race to be accessible to more spectators. Furthermore, we and the city received complaints from residents of the Bronx that we had snubbed their borough by just touching it for a few steps and returning right back to Manhattan. They wanted more of the marathon.

I brought this up with the Traffic Division of the Police Department (the P.D. has a major say because their marathon work comes out of their budget), and they agreed to open up the course for us.

So whereas in 1976 we had laid out a course designed to stay out of trouble, in 1977 we tried to accommodate everybody by putting the course more in the city's mainstream.

In Brooklyn we moved the route away from the isolated Brooklyn Navy Yard and put it on busy Bedford Avenue. In Manhattan we abandoned the inaccessible walkway alongside the East Side Drive and pulled the course inward to go right up First Avenue, through the area known for its vibrant singles bars. We extended the course in the Bronx to a mile and came back to Manhattan on another bridge, the Madison Avenue Bridge, and went directly down Fifth Avenue, all the way to Central Park. That would give us more of Harlem, where the crowds, once feared by some of the white establishment, had in fact been tremendously supportive and spirited. After coming down Central Park's East Drive, we would emerge out of the bottom of the park and cross to the west side of it on 59th Street—Central Park South—which is lined by some of the city's ritziest hotels, the Plaza, the Park Lane, the St. Moritz. Then we would reenter the park at Columbus Circle and finish at our usual place. Now we would be closing 360 intersections and crossing five bridges.

We picked up two new sponsors, Etonic KM running shoes and Perrier, the sparkling water from France which was just launching its American campaign. They joined the original four sponsors, and our budget went up to $100,000. Just after the finish of the 1976 marathon I had noticed that Chris Stewart had his shoes off and his feet were bloody. He said that the jagged steel-mesh walkways on the bridges, especially the long Queensboro Bridge, had cut through his thin racing shoes. Other runners complained, too. So we got a rug company to install on that walkway a blue DuPont Antron carpet 1,300 yards long and forty inches wide—the world's longest carpet. Runners had also complained about the uneven footing on the old cobblestoned section of First Avenue, so we got the city to agree to pave it before the 1977 race.

We doubled the number of ham-radio operators. Our computerized timing and scoring system, with six terminals and two high-speed printers (dwarfed by what we have today), would be the most advanced ever used for a marathon. Block associations and people from the various neighborhoods through which the route passed would help man water stations and other volunteer areas. George Hirsch, at *New Times* magazine, would produce 100,000 copies of the official program.

Everything would be bigger and better. My eyes were on the enticing vistas of that big picture. But suddenly I was waylaid by a small bunch of people who brought my eyes immediately down to earth—to their turf.

I was in my office at the YMCA when my secretary came in, very shaken, tears in her eyes, and said, "There's a bunch of hoodlums out there who demand to see you."

I didn't want to see hoodlums in my office, so I went out to the hallway. There were four kids, maybe seventeen, eighteen years old, in leather jackets and jeans and heavy boots. They looked like something just slightly less menacing than Hell's Angels. The spokesman said he had a few things to say that would straighten me out about my plans for the marathon.

Whatever they had to say, I wanted them to say it right there in front of some of our people who were hanging around, but this stocky guy manhandled me away to a section of the hallway where there wasn't anybody to see us, managing at the same time to let me get a glimpse of the knife stuck in his belt under his jacket. With his buddies surrounding me menacingly, he said he had heard about our plans for a new marathon route using Bedford Avenue in Brooklyn. He said, "Youse ain't gonna run through *our* turf." He said they represented about thirty guys from an apartment-building complex in the area about nine or ten miles into the race, and they weren't going to let our race go through.

My knees began trembling like they did during bombings in the war. I wasn't so scared of them right there, but I was direly spooked about what they could do to the race. I had to hide my fright and buy time while I tried to figure out an angle. I told them to wait a minute, that I had something for them. I went and got a bunch of NYRRC T-shirts. I hand out souvenir T-shirts everywhere I go, and usually it works as well as if I were the

President handing out pens. But I didn't know about this case.

They accepted them silently. But accept them they did. I decided, I won't fight them, I'll try to win them over somehow. I asked the lead guy what was the name of his gang.

"We're not a gang," he said stiffly, "we're protectors of the neighborhood."

That was an opening for me. I said, "Fine, your protection is exactly what we need. We want you to hold your turf for us, and we're not going to assign anybody else to your turf because you can protect it for us better than anybody else." I appointed the four of them special block leaders.

They seemed to mull it over, eyeing me. The leader wrinkled his nose. I held up a finger for them to wait another minute.

I went and got them thirty white windbreakers, our jackets for course marshals. Together with the T-shirts, that seemed to do the trick. They smiled.

After an hour or so of all this macho fencing and posing, we were actually chatting together and laughing like buddies. I told them they had saved our marathon for the whole city of New York.

We shook hands, or thumbs—whatever that grip is—and they left.

A couple of days later they came back and the leader said, "We need more protection in our area, and we gotta get a few supplies." I gave them thirty more windbreakers and a couple hundred dollars. I also gave them some of the club's bicycle caps.

That was the last squeeze they put on me, but I still had no way of feeling secure about the course through their turf. I didn't assign any water stations to them because I didn't trust them with anything to give the runners. For all I knew they could poison the whole pack.

Shortly after that, another bunch came to see me, this one from the Bronx. It was the same thing: We couldn't run on their turf. But this group was younger and tamer. I gave them a bunch of T-shirts and they went away.

I was afraid this could get out of hand, and every gang in the city would start coming out of the woodwork. I was very careful not to let the police or press know because I didn't want anybody to start making moves that would stir things up. Apparently the word never really spread on the street because I never heard from another gang.

For that year we had another terrific field. Bill Rodgers would be back to defend his title, and we had Shorter again. We also had Jerome Drayton, from Canada, who had won the previous Fukuoka Marathon and that year's Boston; we had Finnish runner Lasse Viren, twice a double gold medal winner in the Olympics, taking both the 5,000 meters and 10,000 meters races of 1972 and 1976.

For the women the favorite had to be Kim Merritt, our 1975 winner, who had in September set an American women's record of 2:37:19 in the Nike-Oregon Marathon. And Miki Gorman was back, fresh from a win in Boston.

The day before the race the United Nations hosted a special reception for the international runners, who represented seventeen countries. This event later evolved into our annual International Breakfast Run the morning before marathon day, when all the foreign runners assemble at United Nations Plaza behind their national flags to jog crosstown to Tavern-on-the-Green for a fancy breakfast.

The scene at the staging area at Fort Wadsworth was an even bigger madhouse than before, with 4,823 runners, including 250 women, the most women ever in a marathon. But one small scene within it sticks particularly in my mind. This was publication day for Jim Fixx's *The Complete Book of Running,* which would become a roaring best seller that would make it synonymous with the running boom (and which *People* magazine, years later, would call the most socially provocative book of the decade). Jim was there to run the marathon, and somebody handed him a copy of *The New York Times* in which there was a big, enthusiastic ad for his book. Jim, a gentle, popular guy, had not expected the ad, and as he came up to the starting line, tears were flooding his eyes. Our marathon would be the most perfect celebration.

The field was so large that we abandoned the little starter's pistol and had the Army bring in a 75-mm howitzer on a flatbed truck. Allan Steinfeld coordinated the start. He would give the "go" signal for the lanyard to be pulled on the howitzer. Nobody is a stickler for precision like Allan. A start scheduled for 10:30 would go at 10:30 on the dot. Allan, himself a ham-radio operator, was tracking the exact time by listening to the frequency of the National Bureau of Standards, WWV. When he said "Go!" into his own walkie-talkie and swung his arm down, the timers with ham radios throughout the course, tuned in to Allan's transmission, had the time just as precisely; the howitzer made a "boom" that could be heard across the Narrows in Brooklyn.

From the moment we got across the Verrazano Bridge into Brooklyn, my mind was on the gangs. I had kept it to myself and didn't know what to expect.

When we came to the first of their blocks, there was nobody, not a soul. Either they just took our jackets and disappeared, or worse, maybe they were just waiting to cause trouble somewhere. I scanned the rooftops, half expecting them to be up there ready to pelt us with stones.

Then we made a turn, and suddenly there they were, more than thirty of them, lined up on the sidewalk as if at attention, all in white jackets and bicycle caps. When they saw me in the lead car, they broke into smiles and started waving. The leader yelled out, "Brother Fred, everything's cool, we got you covered!" There was not a single ordinary spectator in the block, just that gang, standing there proud as Marines. We had peace.

(I never saw or heard from them again. The gang from the Bronx never showed up on the course at all.)

We had peace, but suddenly we didn't have press. This year we gave credentials to a lot more press people, so we graduated from a pickup truck to a big old passenger bus to carry them all. The press bus had started out behind us, right in front of the runners, and it had disappeared. Over Steve Mendelsohn's walkie-talkie came the advisory that the old bus had broken down in Queens, and the reporters were scrambling for the subway to get to the finish line.

They would not be happy reporters. If I was lucky, they would blame the bus and not me.

But I didn't have time to dwell on that because suddenly, when we arrived in Manhattan from the Queensboro Bridge and looped around to go up First Avenue, we didn't have our police escort.

Somehow the motorcycle escort had gone straight ahead and ended up on Second Avenue. The crowds on First Avenue completely blocked the running lane. We leaned on the horn, and I ranted and raved for the crowd to make room, but for several blocks we could only inch ahead.

Fortunately (and daringly), Bill Rodgers darted over to the lane on the other side, right amid the moving traffic, and continued his pace. He even passed us. It wasn't until ten blocks later—half a mile—that we finally got reunited with the police escort, got back in front of Rodgers, and put the race together behind us.

The finish line was a joy to behold. The new finish-line system, with its ropes and chutes and timers and scorers, was ready and waiting. It was the first year that we had a few bleachers for the spectator crowd, and two or three thousand of them filled the bleachers. Police security was excellent. And now, rather than let the lead vehicles stop at the finish line and clog everything up, the police efficiently directed them off to the side, through a parking lot, and out of the park.

Security was so tight, in fact, that once out of the park in the lead car I had trouble getting back to the finish line. The cops on duty didn't know me and I hadn't carried identification. I managed to sneak back through the bleacher area.

Rodgers beat Jerome Drayton by almost two and a half minutes, and Chris Stewart was again third, just four seconds behind Drayton. Kim Merritt led a good portion of the women's race but ran out of steam in Central Park. Miki Gorman passed her at twenty-four miles and went on to win by three minutes. Gayle Barron, a TV broadcaster from Atlanta (and next year's

Boston winner), was third. Eight women finished in under three hours, a marathon record.

We were launched, soaring, taking the world by storm, with everybody on our side, loving the marathon. Until 1978. Then we ran into a buzz saw. We got into disputes with the press, the Parks Department, the Police Department, the mayor's office, and a beer company; vandals struck the course; wheelchair athletes took us to court; even UNICEF got into the act. Just when we thought we were getting on top of everything, we were battling politics, publicity, crime, motherhood, and apple pie.

Right from the early days of my presidency of the club, one of my primary efforts was to fill up the dates on our race calendar. I felt the running boom coming. And I noticed that other cities—San Francisco, Los Angeles, Detroit, Buffalo, Chicago—had half a dozen running groups each doing their own thing, with nobody coordinating anything. We wanted the NYRRC to become a unified organization to promote running events in the city for the benefit of the running community and to best promote running. I wanted to control the running events so that not every rinky-dink club could put on a race in Central Park. We had to become the umbrella organization, be recognized as *the* organization in the city for running. To do that, we had to raise operating money and we had to fill in the schedule. There are only so many Saturdays and Sundays, and I wanted them.

One of the things I didn't want was charity races. After the 1977 marathon success we were deluged with requests to put on charity races, and we turned them down. Of course, I'm not against charities. But for the club to exist, we need to have money coming in. If we put on a race with a three-dollar entry fee, we get the three dollars to help cover expenses. And if a race has a corporate sponsor—as 10 to 15 percent of our races do—we can come out ahead and have money to invest in other events and services to fulfill our role as a service organization. But if we put on a race for a charity, not only is there no corporate sponsor but the charity gets the entry fee. They might give us a small service fee of, say, a thousand to put the race on, but you can't run a club like this on money like that. And if you let one charity in, it's impossible to say no to others, and finally every race is a charity race.

That has actually happened in San Francisco and other cities. Ninety percent of the events became charity events, and as a result no single running organization could flourish as ours has.

In the winter of 1978 I heard through the grapevine that UNICEF intended to put on a race of its own in Central Park. UNICEF had hired a public relations agency to promote the race, and they had set a date.

If UNICEF did it, then would come the March of Dimes, and finally there would be a whole season of charity races that would sap our strength and threaten our program, including the marathon.

When I got wind of it, I immediately made up a series of three races, one of them to be on the date UNICEF had chosen. Overnight I got Finnair to sponsor the series, with the overall winner going to Finland to represent New York in the Finlandia Marathon. I hurried over to the Parks Department to shove in my application right away, before UNICEF got around to it. When UNICEF came to the Parks Department, they were informed that the date was already taken. For a big organization like that, which can't act as quickly as we can, to gear up again and find a different date was almost impossible. So they abandoned it.

The Parks Department realized the advantage of having a single strong organization in the city responsible for furthering the cause of running. And by then they recognized us as that organization.

But nobody, including us, wanted to shut out charities entirely. We felt a social obligation and wanted to help in a way that would not distort our program. So since then we have organized one charity event a year—the annual 4-mile New York Benefit Run in July—and all the charities who want to can take part for the benefit fund. That has worked well, and we're the only city in the country that does it this way.

At the opposite end of the spectrum were a couple of beer companies. As a nonprofit organization we're not supposed to make money. But we're not necessarily supposed to lose money either. While every year our budget for the marathon was going up, every year we were losing a good chunk of money on it. The marathon grows, our overall program grows, expenses increase accordingly. In 1977, for example, we had a net loss of about $20,000 for the marathon. Any money we might make from other sponsored races through the season goes toward diminishing that deficit. So we're always scratching for money.

My office was still a cubbyhole at the West Side Y when, in 1978, I got a visit from a public relations executive who said he represented a big company that wanted to be the sole sponsor of the New York City Marathon. At first he didn't name the company. He wanted to know what our budget was. I hemmed and hawed a little, so he said, "Forget the budget, just name your price."

Under such conditions I love picking fat numbers out of the blue—you never know when you might get a bite. I said, "One million dollars."

He said, "Let's discuss it." He said the company would want to use its name in the title of the marathon. They wanted to call it _____'s New York City Marathon.

A beer company. I told him there were two problems: 1) I would never use a beer sponsor for the New York City Marathon; I don't like the image. 2) Nobody will ever preempt the name of our marathon.

He couldn't understand how we could reject that kind of money. And, in fact, I didn't tell anybody at the club about it at the time because I was embarrassed. While we were haggling with one of our sponsors to get $3,000 more out of them, here I was rejecting $1 million. But, trying always to take the long view with regard to money, I was sure I was right.

Later on, I was approached by another beer company, which wanted to sponsor a 10-K race the following year with a huge field of maybe 5,000 runners, and from the proceeds of the race donate $5,000 to each union of three city departments—police, fire, and transit. I didn't want to do it. They said they had already talked to those departments about it and had everybody behind it.

They were putting the squeeze on. I told them the budget for what they were talking about would be $80,000 or $90,000. I thought that would scare them off. It didn't.

Pressure was being felt other places, too. Alice Cashman, who is head of special events for the Parks Department, and one of the most important and supportive people we deal with, said I should try to work something out with these people, see if maybe we could put on the race for them someplace else.

They didn't want it someplace else. They wanted it in Central Park. They kept bugging me for meetings. We were gearing up for the marathon, and I kept avoiding them. We actually set up two appointments, and they brought in heavy hitters from their home office, but I stood them up. That was a mistake. It seemed to make them more fiercely determined. But my mind was on the marathon.

I began getting pressure directly from the unions representing the Police, Fire, and Transit Departments. They were counting on the money from the donations. Even other unions called, supporting them. Everybody was mad at us.

I had guilt feelings because I had stood them up at those meetings. That, combined with the high pressure we were getting, caused me to cave in. Alice Cashman said we'd better go ahead and put it on.

I put the race on the schedule for the following year, with a budget of about $50,000.

When Parks Commissioner Gordon Davis saw that event on the schedule, he blew his stack. Somehow, it seems word about it never reached him until then. Davis, in his first year as commissioner, was not only very capable in his job and an asset to us, he was also very dedicated to keeping the parks pure. He would have nothing to do with a beer sponsorship. So when he found out about it, he was furious and absolutely refused to allow it.

Now it was a real mess. We had agreed to do it, now Commissioner Davis said we couldn't, and he blamed us for agreeing to do it in the first place. But the pressure was on from the unions, and that pressure got to Mayor Ed Koch, who, like any mayor, always had his hands full dealing with the city unions. The pressure circled all the way back to Gordon Davis. Having said no to beer sponsorship, he wasn't going to retract that. But since we'd put it on our schedule, and everybody was all riled up, he said we'd have to go ahead and put on the race ourselves, and pay the promised donations out of our own proceeds.

We couldn't be forced to put on a race, but neither could we afford to alienate the city and its departments. So we put on the race without a sponsor. We made it as simple as possible, a 3-mile "fun run" (which means we don't score it; runners just time themselves). We charged our normal three-dollar fee and got about one thousand runners.

And then we wrote out three $5,000 checks and went down to City Hall, where we presented the checks to the three unions at a ceremony in front of the news media. Allan Steinfeld and I were incredulous at the whole thing. A big, expensive charade. We had to put out $15,000 and eat crow on top of it.

But, then, that is part of the price you pay for being the premier organization for running in the city.

6

The most difficult issue we ever faced was the controversy over wheelchairs. It has dogged us for eight years and is not fully dead yet. There's no way to put such an emotional issue gently to rest. We opposed having wheelchairs in our marathon. How can you argue against wheelchairs? Despite our pioneering efforts to include women, to promote running for inner-city kids, to provide a program for prison inmates, and our sponsorship of handicapped running classes and the Achilles Track Club (for handicapped runners *including* wheelchair athletes), our stand against wheelchairs in the main event cast us as ogres.

It all started quietly enough in 1976. A month before the marathon I got a call from Bob Hall, a wheelchair athlete from Boston who had raced in the Boston Marathon (which accepts wheelchair racers, giving them a fifteen-minute head start). He wanted me to invite him to run in New York and pay his expenses. I explained that while we did accept handicapped runners—such as Dick Traum, who runs on an artificial leg—I drew the line at wheelchairs. I said no, and that was that.

But in 1977 Hall and a few other wheelchair athletes began lobbying for me to accept them. We called a meeting to hear them out. It was a relatively friendly two-hour session. Naturally, we were sympathetic to their wish to participate in sports and not be discriminated against. But our club officers—such as Traum and Ted Corbitt, who, as a physical therapist for disabled people, worked continually with wheelchair-bound athletes—were firm against including them in the marathon.

First of all, our marathon is a foot race, not a bicycle race or a roller-skate race or a wheelchair race. My job is to promote and develop the sport of foot racing, like somebody else's job might be for skydiving or figure skating.

Second, there is the safety issue. Wheelchairs can go thirty to forty miles per hour on downhills, and the speed disparity can create a real hazard for foot racers. Our course included steep ramps and narrow walkways, and space was tight—we were already having to reject hundreds of runners because we couldn't accommodate them safely. Collisions between wheelchairs and runners would be inevitable. Dick Traum, who lost his leg in an accident and spent a long time in a wheelchair before being fitted with an artificial leg, said that a wheelchair could be a "lethal weapon" in a footrace.

Still, nobody could deny that it's a thrill and inspiration to see disabled athletes complete a marathon. So instead of including them in our footrace marathon, I proposed to conduct a Wheelchair Marathon Championship in Central Park. Mayor Koch agreed to it, and I even got Manufacturers Hanover Trust to agree to sponsor it. That was rejected. Hall took the matter to court.

Two days before the 1977 marathon, State Supreme Court Justice Arnold Fraiman dismissed Hall's case on a technicality, without ruling on the basic issue. But then Justice Fraiman called me to urge that I avoid bad publicity by letting Hall enter anyway.

So I let Hall in and gave him a twenty-minute head start. He was wearing an official number, but we didn't include him in the official scoring.

That was not the end of it. In 1978 it really hit the fan. Hall and another wheelchair athlete, Curtis Brinkman, applied for the marathon and we rejected them. The state's Human Rights Division began making inquiries. I didn't want to talk to them.

Mayor Koch got upset with us and put out a press release in support of wheelchairs in the marathon.

Parks Commissioner Davis was angry, too, because he had received a lot of pressure from the mayor's office and other groups, and not only were we causing him grief but we were wrong. He told me we had to accept wheelchairs.

I had been stalling the Human Rights Division because if we were going to have to fight about such a sensitive matter, I preferred to take the matter to a regular court, fight it out there, and have it settled once and for all. I said to Davis, "Are you afraid that if we left it up to a court, we would win?" He said, "I don't care if you win or lose in court, I am *ordering* you to accept them. You're going to accept wheelchairs or there's not going to be a marathon."

"If you cancel the marathon," I said, "I'll resign."

He left me with his ultimatum, and I left him with mine. I was bluffing a little. I don't know if he was.

One day at the end of September I got a chilly visit from Evelyn Goodman, representing the state's Human Rights Division. She said she had come to see me about the marathon applications from Bob Hall and Curt Brinkman, and she demanded to see our list of accepted runners for the 1978 race. I told her the list could not be shown to the public. She said, "I am not the public, Mr. Lebow."

I told her I couldn't do anything about it immediately but that I'd have our lawyer, Bennett Gershman, contact her.

Right after that, the Human Rights Division itself filed a court suit charging me and the NYRRC with discriminating against disabled people in a place of public accommodation—i.e., the streets where we ran the marathon. The court handed down an injunction saying that we couldn't bar Hall and Brinkman from participating in the 1978 marathon unless I appeared to show cause why they should be barred.

Well, the marathon is bigger than I, the parks commissioner, the mayor, and the wheelchair athletes put together, so I decided not to fight it right then, just before the marathon. I agreed to accept Hall and Brinkman as official entrants.

Still the matter wasn't put to rest, though, because at the same time I received a subpoena to appear at hearings before the Human Rights Division. There were four days of hearings at the division offices in the World Trade Center.

Several wheelchair athletes and friends testified in support of wheelchairs. The most prominent name among them was Bill Rodgers (Bob Hall worked in his running store in Boston). Rodgers had the strongest of sympathies for wheelchair athletes; he felt they should be allowed to compete in marathons right up through the Olympics, even though the best of the wheelchair racers could complete a marathon several minutes faster than the best marathon runner. (I never doubted Billy's sincerity in this matter, but at this point, when we were haggling over prize money for his participation as well, it certainly didn't help our relationship.)

Witnesses for us included Dick Traum, Ted Corbitt, and run-ner-author Jim Fixx. Gary Bullock, a good marathoner, told of being hit by a wheelchair and knocked out of our previous marathon. Vince Chiappetta, then cochairman of the National AAU Long-Distance Running Committee, called attention to the AAU rules, which stated: "No athlete may participate" in AAU events (of which our marathon was one) "if they are aided by implements which are used for locomotion; by wheels or skids or any other device . . . (e.g. wheelchair, skateboards, etc.). . . . "

While I resented being characterized by the division's lawyer as somebody who "hated" wheelchairs, what angered me most was Bob Hall himself. Whereas Curt Brinkman was a double amputee who was in fact wheelchair-bound, it came out in the hearings that Hall, a polio victim, could walk and even jog, unaided. (Liz Levy, then a top New York runner, told me she danced with Hall after the Bermuda Marathon.) He used a wheelchair to compete in athletic events, such as road races and basketball games. He even admitted in the hearings that he could probably complete a marathon on his feet but that it would take him five or six hours, and he wouldn't subject himself to that because he wasn't "a masochist."

It galled me that a guy who didn't even *need* a wheelchair for ordinary locomotion was using the issue as a personal platform, and the media was playing right into it. There's only so much publicity the marathon can get, and I want that to be for the runners. In those days we were fighting for every inch of space we could get in the newspapers. When I saw news from other cities, the most prominent marathon pictures were always of wheelchairs. And why not? They are very dramatic. But I felt that took away from the runners, from the sport. Now Hall was getting a lot of publicity for himself by picking on me and our marathon.

But none of this mattered much. I felt that the issue before the Human Rights Division was essentially emotional. Although *The New York Times* supported our position in an editorial, we were really in a no-win situation.

Personally, I was taking a beating. A lot of people advised me to give in on it and forget about it. They feared the club and I were going to be severely burned by the wheelchair issue.

And I must say, there were times when I felt like crawling into a hole. It was a terrible position to be in, to be opposed to people so disadvantaged, for what might have seemed to be selfish purposes. But in my mind it was not selfish; it was for thousands and thousands of runners.

It would have been much easier to give in, even though I felt strongly about it. A lot of race directors did give in, while at the same time privately encouraging me and hoping we'd win so as to make it easier for them to adopt our position. It would have been nice if some of them had come forward publicly. We were in a lonely place.

In June 1979 the Human Rights Division ruled against us, asserting that we were guilty of practicing discrimination. We appealed to the Human Rights Appeal Board and lost, as expected.

So then we took the issue to the State Supreme Court—a thankless task for our able lawyer, Bennett Gershman—and there we won. The Human Rights Division appealed to the state's highest court, the State Court of Appeals.

Finally, in February 1982, the State Court of Appeals upheld the lower court, and us, in a 5–1 ruling saying that our marathon rules "required participants to use only their feet, and not wheel-chairs, skateboards, bicycles or other extraneous aids" and that our rules did not "constitute an unlawful discriminatory practice."

Shortly after the 1982 ruling, Parks Commissioner Davis, by request of Mayor Koch, wrote to a lawyer representing the Eastern Paralyzed Veterans Association to say that the Court of Appeals decision "in no way alters the city's position" regarding participation of wheelchairs in our marathon.

In practice, we and the city have not been so far apart. We have operated with kind of a tacit agreement; everything is low-key.

With the 1982 marathon approaching, Alice Cashman, of the Parks Department, leaned on me to accept two wheelchair applicants. I made a compromise with her: I would accept one but not the other. The other was Bob Hall. I said I would not accept Bob Hall because he did not meet the requirements of a wheelchair-bound athlete. She accepted the compromise.

Back in 1978, when all this was just heating up, we still had a marathon to put on. We had accepted the unbelievable total of 11,400 entrants—more than double the previous year—and had to reject 5,000. Instead of using just one side of the divided Verrazano Bridge, as in previous years, we would now use both sides. The veteran male runners would start on one side; to their left the other start would be for first-time men and all women, with the elite women up front to give them a clearer start and chance to develop their early pace in less of a crowd, before both halves merged together two and a half miles into the race. (How crucial a clear start would be we didn't then realize; a women's world record was coming up.)

For more efficient scoring of this massive field, Allan Steinfeld and his committee had developed a system of bar codes, like those on supermarket items. The bar codes, corresponding to the runners' numbers, were stapled to the big printed numbers the runners pinned on their T-shirts, and at the end of the finish-line chutes the bar codes would be snatched off, spindled, and messengered back to the data-entry trailer to be read by hand-held electronic scanners—replacing the manual system of writing the numbers down as the runners came through the chutes.

We increased our medical personnel along the course and at the finish to three hundred and our total volunteer staff to three thousand. We used several floors of the former Huntington Hartford Museum, a ten-story structure on Columbus Circle, as our marathon headquarters.

I felt this was really to be our "show-off" year. We were big and splashy, fat with talent and experience. CBS television cameras would record segments for the news; several press helicopters would hover over the race. We had not only the world's best male marathoner, Bill Rodgers, but the women's world-record holder, West Germany's Christa Vahlensieck. Challenging Vahlensieck would be Martha Cooksey from California, the Avon International Champion, who believed she had a good shot at cracking the 2:34:48 world record. We had a strong, deep field of elite runners to push the favorites.

If we were looking for omens, though, they started at the start and never stopped. The omens were bad news.

From the open back of the Subaru "Brat" lead car (provided and driven by the president of the distributor), I looked back at a sea of eleven thousand runners at the starting line, tensed, leaning forward in anticipation of the cannon's boom.

Mayor Koch pulled the lanyard of the howitzer. Nothing happened. He pulled it again. Nothing. Only then did it occur to everybody that the gun was empty. A soldier stepped up with the dummy shell and loaded the gun. The starting "boom" was a minute late. I imagined Allan screaming.

At the nine-mile point in Brooklyn, Rodgers was in an early duel with Garry Bjorklund, an Olympic 10,000-meter finalist from Minneapolis who had pushed Rodgers early last year and was Billy's main concern this year.

My main concern was what I heard over the radio. The police up ahead called in to say there were two blue lines at the fourteen-mile point in Queens and wanted to know which line we should follow. I was momentarily befuddled by such a message. They said some people had painted a fake blue line during the night, leading off from our real blue line. A precinct captain had discovered two men and a woman painting the line and had arrested them. The problem now was that one line went straight ahead and one made a sharp right turn, and they didn't know which was the fake. "Take the sharp right turn!" I directed to Steve Mendelsohn, who relayed it over the radio. I could only hope the whole field followed.

A motorcycle cop roared up from behind, and he yelled to me, "The press bus is too close to the runners. They're killing the runners with fumes!" The two big Sanitation Department trucks carrying photographers were positioned okay, but the bus was not. I told Mendelsohn to get the bus on the radio. A ham operator was now in every vehicle. Except the press bus. Somebody had thrown the ham off the bus to make more room. Over the noise of the motorcycle and the crowd and the radios I tried to make the cop understand that I wanted him to go back and move the bus up closer to the lead car, away from the pack. He slowed and drifted back. I grabbed a piece of paper and wrote a big sign: "JOE—STAY AWAY FROM THE RUNNERS," and waved it at the bus, where our public relations man, Joey Goldstein, was riding.

The next thing I knew, the bus turned off the course and was gone. The motorcycle cop was back, yelling to me that he had thrown the bus off the course. I couldn't believe it. Last year the press bus broke down, now this. There would be hell to pay next time the reporters got hold of me, plus we were losing coverage of the race. "Why? Why?" I cried, as the cop roared away.

The motorcycle cops escorting the marathon—the same guys who escort the President when he comes to town—have an iron rule that we encourage: Anybody interferes with the runners, they move or get bounced. The cop must have misunderstood me. Who the hell threw the damn ham off the press bus?

Minutes later—we still hadn't reached the halfway point in Queens—I got word that the cops had made an alteration in the course where we come back from the Bronx into Manhattan.

We sped up to a police car carrying some brass. "You can't make that change!" I yowled. "Please, please, the times will be all wrong! You are ruining the marathon! We had a *deal!*"

This year we had outgrown the walkways on the bridges leading into and out of the Bronx. We needed the roadways. The Police Department couldn't accept the idea of tying up bridge traffic for three hours. We had made a compromise: In exchange for the roadways, the course coming off the bridge back into Manhattan would be altered slightly to take it away from the line of bridge traffic. But when we recalibrated the course, it was 159 yards too long. Two nights before the marathon I had an urgent meeting with Chief John Schawaroch of the P.D. Traffic Division. Parks Commissioner Davis was there, and he thought I was overreacting. "You don't have to tell anybody the course is longer," Davis said. "Who would know?"

"I would know," I had said. So I made another compromise with the P.D.: We would have the roadway for an hour, then the cops could move the rest of the field back onto the walkway; and we'd eliminate the alteration that made the course too long.

Now, it seemed, the cops had for some reason reverted to the plan that made the course too long. Not only would the timing for the whole race be a shambles, but any possible record set would be voided because of the mismeasured course.

No sooner had I lapsed into despair about that than the police car returned, and the officer called, "Okay, Fred, you got it back."

Another crisis past. How many more were lurking? I felt I couldn't take any more.

Somewhere between fifteen and seventeen miles, Bill Rodgers put Garry Bjorklund away and surged to a lead that would bring him his third straight win. But I was thinking only of the course. We sped up and moved away from the race to see what was in store.

First Avenue was fine, excellent, more cops, more barricades, more space. There were tears of joy and relief in my eyes because Chief Schawaroch had done such a superb job with his cops. The bridges were fine. The whole rest of the course was fine.

But not the finish. We arrived to find the finish-line area in chaos. Crowds had spilled out of the bleachers and were all over the place. I had urged the cops to pay more attention to First Avenue, which they had, and now there weren't enough of them at the finish to maintain security.

I ordered my car to stop and I jumped out, frantic to bring some order.

Instead of proceeding off the course and out of the way, the driver pulled the Subaru right up to the finish line and parked it there. "Get that car out of there!" I screamed, running over.

"You said I could leave it at the finish line," he said.

"I didn't! Move it!" Bill Rodgers would be in sight any moment.

"I've got a right to be here!" he yelled back. "We made a contract for five thousand dollars!"

"You can take the five thousand and shove it!"

He moved the car, and I plunged into the finish-line mess and started pushing people out of the way. We cleared a path for Rodgers to come across, and then I went to work clearing the chutes for the rest of the runners. A press helicopter swooped too low, sending debris whirling up from the road into everybody's eyes. I screamed at the helicopter.

I was still shoving spectators and press people away from the rear of the chutes so the runners could be scored when it dawned on me that I had completely forgotten the women's race. Men were filling the chutes, and it was time for the women's winner.

The crowd in the bleachers was cheering encouragement for somebody. I dashed back to the finish line.

A hundred yards down the course, Martha Cooksey was on her knees, struggling to get up. A couple of men trotted out to help her, but she waved them away. Allan Steinfeld hovered near her, making sure none of the well-meaning spectators aided her and caused her to be disqualified. She got up, staggered almost to the finish line, sank to her hands and knees, and crawled across. Her time was 2:41:48. She was announced as finishing second.

But, then, who won?

"Some blond girl," somebody said. "Number 1173, I think. She wasn't listed in the program."

"What time?" I asked.

"I think it was 2:32:30."

That was a *world record,* by more than *two minutes!* Some blond girl, not in the program—a late entry. It must have been Grete! It was impossible. Grete Waitz had never run a marathon before in her life!

It was Grete. Nobody had known who she was when she crossed the finish line, and now nobody could find her. She had disappeared.

How Grete Waitz, a twenty-five-year-old schoolteacher from Oslo, Norway, happened to run the New York City Marathon— and then went on to become one of the greatest long-distance runners of all time—is a story of misunderstandings, ignorance, and luck.

A month or so before the marathon, Finnair, our former sponsor, contacted us with the suggestion that we invite Grete Waitz to run our marathon. Except for people who follow international track results, Grete was unknown in this country. But she was the reigning World Cup 3,000-meter champion and World Cross Country champion and had run the year's fastest women's mile in the world in 4:26:9—all in Europe. She was the world's best middle-distance runner. She was a track runner, not a road runner, but she would still be a good name to have in our field. Since she was totally inexperienced at the distance, I doubted that she would finish the marathon. But with her middle-distance speed, even if she dropped out at the halfway point, she could set an early pace hot enough to pull people behind her like Vahlensieck and Cooksey and propel them into perhaps a record time. So we invited her, and she accepted.

A couple of weeks later I was getting a routine late-night briefing from the woman who then handled our invitations to elite runners. Among the matters she mentioned was that she had withdrawn the invitation to Grete. Grete had contacted her to say she wanted to bring her husband, Jack. She had never been to New York, and because of recent disappointments in races, she was thinking of retiring from running altogether; she was coming to New York only at the urging of her husband, to experience a marathon and have a chance to visit New York City before her running career was over. So she would come only if she could bring her husband.

We had a general rule that we don't pay expenses for husbands or wives of invited runners. So our woman in charge of invitations had rejected Grete's request and Grete would not be coming.

Automatically, I said okay—we were going down a list of many items, and I wasn't giving it any thought.

A few minutes later it hit me: Grete Waitz! Of course I wanted her! Of course she could bring her husband! We sent a telex immediately, reinstating her.

I first met her at Tavern-on-the-Green, at a premarathon reception hosted by Finnair. There was no special interest in her, no press hanging around her. I introduced myself, and we chatted. I knew she had never run a marathon, but I assumed she had put in some heavy mileage for this, her first. I asked her what was the longest distance she had ever run.

"Twenty kilometers," she said.

Only twelve and a half miles! I was taken aback. Even ordinary competitors typically put in a few runs of twenty miles or so in preparation for a marathon. She won't even be a rabbit, I thought, she won't last long enough.

As I said, I couldn't find her immediately after the race. I didn't see her until the awards ceremony that night. Now everybody was hovering around her. She was an instant celebrity. The press was trying to find out everything about her—how she trained, what her running records were, what she did for a living—pronouncing her name all kinds of ways but right (it's "Vites"). She was answering questions graciously, unpretentiously, shyly, quietly—never mentioning the awesome trial she'd been through to complete the race. Finally I got a chance to congratulate her and tell her it was an incredible performance.

Only years later did I find out how incredible it *really* had been. Those who saw her cross the finish line thought they were looking at a woman running with efficient ease, even though setting a world record. They couldn't have been more wrong. But

Grete is so reserved in talking about herself that she never even told me what she had been through until this year.

In the latter stages of that race, Grete told me, she had begun to hurt. With our course marked by miles and not kilometers, as she was used to—plus her unfamiliarity with the marathon distance—she was disoriented about the distance left to run. When she entered Central Park, she was in terrible pain throughout her body, wracked with exhaustion. Had she known she still had three miles to go, she told me, she would have quit, dropped out. But she kept thinking that the finish line had to be just over the next hill, just around the next curve.

When she finally finished, she didn't know she had set a record. She didn't even know what the marathon record *was*. She just remembered yelling at her husband: He was to blame for putting her through such agony! She would never do anything like this again!

The reason nobody could find her right after her finish was that she had gone directly back to her hotel to lie down—she hurt too much to talk to anybody. Then word came to her that she had set a world record in this, her first marathon. Slowly the significance sank in. After resting awhile, she went to the evening awards ceremony, where she received the plaudits due her from everybody, including me.

Aside from asking to bring her husband that first time, Grete has never asked us for anything. Except once: After that first awards ceremony, she asked for twenty dollars so she could take a cab to the airport.

Because of her amazing success in her first marathon, Grete did not retire. The 1978 victory and world record would be just the first of many incredible performances in an incredible new career as a marathoner. In her second marathon, 1979 New York, she broke her own world record; in her third, 1980 New York, she broke the record again. Through 1983 she won every marathon she finished (she had to drop out of one New York and one Boston with injuries), including the first World Championship Marathon in Helsinki in 1983, and set four world marathon records. No other marathoner has achieved such a level of consistent supremacy. She came to dominate women's road racing at distances from ten kilometers to the marathon to a degree that neither she (who called herself "a track runner who occasionally runs marathons" until 1983, when she called herself "a marathoner") nor anyone else could have dreamed before she flashed, unknown, across the finish line in New York in 1978.

Well, the 1978 race had been splendid all around. In fact, at the awards ceremony Chief Schawaroch, of the N.Y.P.D. Traffic Division, got a standing ovation—the biggest ovation of the night—for the excellence his cops had shown in controlling the crowds on First Avenue. It left him deeply moved; cops don't get standing ovations from the public. Tears had come to my eyes when I entered First Avenue during the race and saw the great job the cops had done; tears came to Chief Schawaroch's eyes now.

There was one more set of damp eyes, though, for an unfortunate reason. Accolades were passed out from the stage to everyone who made a significant contribution to this year's latest success, the biggest marathon of all time. With one exception. Allan Steinfeld—who left the teaching profession to work at lower pay for us, who slaved night and day in the creation, precision, and execution of the intricate technical systems that allowed the race to succeed and have today its first world record—received no mention at all.

Allan never seeks the limelight. But this time the technical director of the marathon left the hall crushed, trying to hide his tears.

It was an unwitting slight by the master of ceremonies. But it served as an important reminder to me that no matter how good the systems are, it will always be the dedicated people who make them work; and it is crucial to acknowledge them, never take them for granted.

The irony was, nobody in our club is more attentive than Allan to the detail of giving recognition for effort.

7

We now entered a new era for marathons: the age of national television. We sold the television rights for live two-hour coverage of the 1979 marathon to "Marathon Entertainment," a New York–based independent syndication company put together for this purpose by Allen Lubell. We didn't get huge money—around $25,000, about what the Rudin family had given us to launch the five-borough marathon in 1976—but that wasn't important. What was important was that fifty stations across the country would carry the broadcast. It would be the first live broadcast of any marathon outside of the Olympics. Ultimately, it would be television more than anything else that would put us on the top of the heap in the international limelight.

Another innovation, less dramatic but significant, also involved cameras. We installed three videotape cameras at our finish line. Allan went to Honolulu to speak at an international meeting of race directors and learned that the Honolulu Marathon used videotape at its finish line. It would be a good idea for us. He got Leo Hoarty, a computer consultant at the United Nations, to install the rented cameras.

Primarily, the cameras were to serve as a double-check, a backup for our scoring system. It is always possible for someone to miss being scored, or to be scored wrong, in the chutes—a bar

Start of the 1978 New York City Marathon at the Verrazano
Narrows Bridge *(Janeart Ltd.)*

(From left) Harrison J. Goldin, Carol Bellamy, Alberto Salazar, Alli
Roe, Mayor Ed Koch, and Charlie McCabe of Manufacturers Hanov
Trust after the 1981 New York City Marathon, in which Salazar and
Roe each set a new world record *(© Lisa Osta)*

'red Lebow *(center, rear)* 'ith his mother, older rother, sister, and baby rother in Arad, Rumania

In more carefree days before Nazi and Russian occupations of World War II, Fred Lebow, thirteen, cruised his hometown of Arad, Rumania, on his bicycle.

'red Lebow with Pope John Paul II in Rome, 1982. *(Paul J. Sutton/Duomo)*

Fred Lebow with Grete Waitz, checking out the course for the World Country Championships
(Gloria Averbuch)

Harry Murphy *(left)* and Ted Corbitt at the NYRRC awards banquet, January 1981
(© Lisa Osta)

harlie McCabe and Barbara Paddock of Manufacturers Hanover Trust
t the start of the 1983 New York City Marathon *(Julie Betts Testwuide)*

Geoff Smith *(forefront)* and Rod Dixon at New York's Columbus Circle approximately 300 yards from the finish line of the 1983 marathon, just before Dixon passed to win *(Patricia L. Owens)*

Thirteen seconds after crossing the finish line, Rod Dixon praises the skies for his 1983 victory while collapsed second-place finisher Geoff Smith awaits medical attention. *(New York Daily News Photo)*

Commissioner Henry J. Stern presents flowers to Ann Audin, winner of the 1983 L'eggs Mini Marathon. Audin is flanked by second-place winner Grete Waitz *(left)* and third-place winner Nancy Rooks of Canada. *(Calvin Wilson)*

Two days after the 1983 New York City Marathon, winners Rod Dixon, Grete Waitz, and one-legged finisher John Paul Cruz, accompanied by Fred Lebow, were guests of President Ronald Reagan in the Oval Office. *(White House Photo)*

code can be lost or misplaced in position; an injured runner might be taken to the medical area without going through the chute, and attendants might forget to remove the bar code for scoring. There are always some mistakes. But with a videotape camera covering each of the three finish-line sections for the entire race, every finisher will appear on the tape as he or she passes under the clock, so mistakes or omissions can be corrected.

In 1979 the cameras came to serve in an equally important, but opposite, function: for what they didn't see. It was the time of Rosie Ruiz. By the following year she would become the focus of the biggest national story in the history of the marathon.

We also entered another era: the first year when applications for the marathon soared to more than double what we could accept. We raised our acceptances to fourteen thousand, but we had to reject thousands of others. Suddenly just getting *into* the New York City Marathon was a major hurdle. By 1983 we would have to reject more than two thirds of the applications; bribe offers, ruses, scalping of marathon numbers, and heart-rending pleas for acceptance would be commonplace and a major element in stories about the marathon.

At the time, this caught us by surprise. Even though the marathon had been expanding explosively, still the meager beginnings were very recent history. The idea that just four years after struggling to launch the city-wide marathon we would be struggling to *contain* it was mind-boggling.

We've always had trouble with the start, and the difficulty increased with the size of the field. We've never found a completely satisfactory way to get everybody organized. There are pace signs alongside the starting field spaced from front to back—"5 Minutes," "6 Minutes," on back to "10 Minutes"—and the runners are supposed to group themselves more or less behind the sign that indicates the minutes-per-mile pace they expect to run. The field should line up in order of descending speed, so the faster runners won't be held up by, or mow down, the slower ones. But the most difficult part is right at the front, which we try to restrict to elite runners only—the very fastest.

There are always a lot of runners trying to mix in with the elite at the front, either to get a better start or to be where the press and TV cameras are.

One problem is the sheer mass of runners. Another problem is time. We bring the runners up from Fort Wadsworth just fifteen minutes before the start, because once they get up there they want to run, and the longer we hold them, the more uncontrollable they get. Everybody pushes forward; it is all we can do to get the front of the pack behind the starting-line tape, which is put down on the roadway. We have marshals who physically push the mob back.

We've never found a way to solve this turmoil efficiently. We don't want to use police because that's not a good image. (In Boston the top finishers run into the arms of police, who escort them away from the finish line; in New York, only our own personnel have direct involvement with the runners, start and finish.) In Paris they do two interesting things at the start. They have a huge water spray from a fire hose sending a high-pressure stream across the front so nobody can advance across the line ahead of time; they separate the elite runners by stationing behind them, between the elite and the rest of the field, about one hundred members of the Club Français running organization, all locking arms.

I don't want to use a fire hose—that's a rather hostile-looking sight for television—but I've toyed with the idea of having a bunch of big runners locking arms behind the elite runners. The difficulty with that is finding big runners who, once the cannon goes off, can run fast enough to keep from obstructing the rest of the field.

In any event, in 1979, on a humid morning so foggy that you couldn't see the top of the bridge, we had this barely manageable field of twelve thousand runners we were trying to get organized at the starting line. We experimented with stringing a rope across the front to keep everybody behind the line, but the elite runners quickly rejected that, fearing they might get tangled up in it.

I was in the lead car, looking back at the pack, ready for the start, and things didn't look good. The front rank looked unruly. We had more foreign runners than ever before—about twelve hundred, from thirty-nine countries—and a lot of them were up front. They looked very jittery. I was especially nervous about the South Americans. The biggest South American race, the New Year's Eve, Midnight Run in São Paulo, Brazil, is notorious for runners jumping the gun at the start. I had a bullhorn, but the sound didn't carry far enough loud enough for me to calm them down.

I watched Allan. That year we had a countdown. It was the last year we had a countdown. It was a big mistake. A countdown lets the runners anticipate and practically dares them to jump the gun.

Allan barked, "Ten, nine, eight . . ."

All of a sudden, a single runner sprinted forward, and a stampede erupted behind him. A sea of runners burst upon us, engulfing the lead vehicles before we could move. In the midst of this the cannon fired. Somehow, Bill Rodgers and Frank Shorter and some other elite runners had managed to hold their marks (avoiding disqualification) until the "boom." Now they too were trapped in the wave. Shorter angrily slapped my car as he went by; runners were briefly pinned against the press bus as it started to move. I was sure somebody would be trampled or run over; anybody falling in this melee could be killed.

Reflexively I blamed the South Americans for the false start, thinking of São Paulo. I had the rash thought that I would never again allow foreigners in our marathon.

But the false start had been caused by a reporter for the tabloid *New York Post*. A very slow marathoner, he had sneaked into the front rank and jumped the gun—by predesign with his photographers—so they could run a big picture of him in front the next day and he could say in his story: "For one glorious moment, the marathon was mine. I led the field for the first hundred yards."

(It could have got somebody killed, let alone how it screwed up the clocks and computers and everything else. I disqualified him permanently, but later he came and apologized profusely, saying his editors had asked him to do it; he made all kinds of amends, wrote favorable running articles, and helped at our races. So after a year's suspension, I removed the lifetime disqualification.)

Gradually, the vehicles edged forward through the throng to the front, and the race formed properly behind them. The photographers' truck, though, got stuck so far back that it detoured through Brooklyn to pass the race and rejoin the lead convoy after ten miles.

Bill Rodgers was buried in the pack, behind maybe 150 runners, and for quite a while radio traffic crackled with the question "Where's Rodgers?"

Kirk Pfeffer, a fast but relatively inexperienced marathoner from Colorado, took a huge lead. By the halfway point he was on a world-record pace and ahead of the lead pack by five hundred yards. For twenty three miles Pfeffer led.

But he had spent himself with the early pace and slowed dramatically. Rodgers caught him just inside Central Park. That Billy somehow worked his way through the tangled field and came on to win his fourth straight New York was amazing. Not his fastest, but perhaps his best race ever, given the start.

The live television was, unfortunately, a partial bust. For most of the race the fog and technical failures allowed only sporadic signals to be relayed from the TV car to the two helicopters and back to the studio. Sportscaster Bill Mazer and sidekick Marty Liquori, the onetime mile champion, did their best without pictures. Coverage was restored in time to show Rodgers overtaking Pfeffer and winning. But by then the broadcast had run out of time, and it was off the air when Grete Waitz finished with her second world record in 2:27:33—an incredible five minutes faster than her first record the year before.

Still, TV ground was broken for us and would be with our race to stay.

Our cameras at the finish line, on the other hand, continued to whir. The videotape recorded the entire field as it crossed the finish line. And that was important. Our bar-code system, the primary system, recorded the finish of a Cuban-born twenty-six-year-old woman named Rosie Ruiz, wearing number W907, in a time of 2:56:29, putting her in twenty-fourth place among the women.

That the pitiful saga of Rosie Ruiz should unfold at the subsequent Boston Marathon was ironic.

The wonderful, staid, old Boston Marathon—oldest in the country, the most prestigious, for so long the *only* marathon of any count. The Boston Marathon was already seventy-three years old when we held our first New York City Marathon in 1970. As the recent marathon boom mushroomed around it, the Boston Athletic Association tried to keep its marathon what it was— steadfastly amateur, noncommercial, properly New England traditional. It wouldn't even pay runners' expenses, let alone prize money. But in 1981, the BAA, in an attempt to bring the marathon into competitive status with upstarts like ourselves, got entangled in some newfangled commercial ideas and contracted with a promoter-lawyer named Marshall Medoff to bring in commercial sponsorship from which Medoff would get a hefty piece of the action. Reaction is what the deal got. Bostonians rebelled at the notion of such pandering for their hallowed marathon. Medoff produced nine sponsors for their 1982 race, and after that Boston wanted no more of it. The BAA sued to void the contract, and in August 1983 the Superior Court in Boston did just that, giving control back to the BAA. (There may be more appeals before the issue is totally resolved.)

But in 1980, though less than half our size, the Boston Marathon was still the grand old Boston Marathon, and Will Cloney, the director since 1946, who would retire in 1982 under fire over the Medoff affair, was still the grand old man of directors.

In April Allan and I went back to Boston to witness the annual Patriot's Day event. Bill Rodgers won, and we waited for the women's winner, expecting it to be either Patti Lyons, of Boston, or Jacqueline Gareau, from Montreal, whom on-course reports had as being the leaders.

Then suddenly across the finish line came a woman with an ungainly stride, tall, fleshier than a typical elite runner, with short dark hair, wearing number W50. She fell into the arms of two cops, who escorted her away from the finish line. A few seconds later I was stunned to hear the announcement: Rosie Ruiz, *from New York,* had won the women's race in a time of 2:31:56—only half a minute off the American-record time.

I was standing about ten feet away from Will Cloney, the race director. Immediately I walked over to him and said, "Will, there's something wrong. I've never seen this woman before, never heard of her." He was oblivious. Even as late as 1980, Boston, which tried to throw out Kathy Switzer in 1967 and didn't accept women officially until 1972 (when our Nina Kuscsik won), still didn't pay much attention to women runners.

On the victory stand Ruiz was crowned with a laurel wreath and held up her arms in a victory salute. Her T-shirt wasn't even sweaty. She didn't look at all like a top-flight runner, and I couldn't believe there was a top runner from New York whom I didn't know—unless she didn't do her running in New York.

If I was stunned at the finish, I was more deeply shocked, appalled, to learn at the following press conference that Ruiz had qualified for Boston (women qualified by running a previous marathon in 3:10 or better; New York has no qualifying time) by running the previous New York City Marathon in a time of 2:56:29. It was impossible. Suddenly, out of the blue, *our* credibility was on the line.

Allan went immediately to a pay phone to call our New York office for a check on the Ruiz claim.

In front of the press I asked Ruiz: Are you a member of the New York Road Runners Club? "No." Any other club? "No." Do you have a coach? "No." She insisted she trained about sixty-five miles a week, running around the Central Park reservoir. More questions: Do you run intervals in training (alternating slow and fast paces)? "What's an interval?" What was your ten-mile split (time at the ten-mile mark)? "What's a split?"

Allan came back. "Fred," he said, "we got problems."

He had talked to Alice Schneider at the NYRRC office, and she had quickly punched up the name on the computer. Rosie Ruiz had indeed been recorded as finishing our marathon in 2:56:29. The data on her entry information also revealed that New York had been her first marathon ever, and under "Predicted Time" for our marathon she had written "4:10," a reasonable expectation for a first-time marathoner.

I didn't know how she got into our computer as a top New York finisher, but she was a fraud. I labeled her that publicly right then and there, to anybody who would listen. Boston officials were more cautious. Will Cloney didn't want to "jump to any conclusions." I said, "Will, cheating in New York is bad enough; cheating in Boston is sacrilegious." The Boston press wasn't very interested. They didn't pursue Ruiz.

I did. That afternoon a *New York Post* reporter and I went to her hotel room. Two stern-looking women let us in. Rosie was propped up on the bed: heavy thighs, folds in her stomach—no way she was a runner. It was even more obvious than before. We chatted briefly. Then I said: "Now that it's all over, Rosie, don't you think it's time to admit that you made a mistake?" She got teary-eyed. I felt she was on the verge of admitting the truth and that she wanted to.

The other two women gruffly asked us to leave.

I returned to New York deeply troubled. We had a major fraud on our hands, but I didn't have any pieces of the puzzle. Who was she? Did she actually run in our race and finish? If not, how did her "time" get into our computer?

A girl came into my office at the West Side Y, all smiles. "Isn't it wonderful," she said, "that the woman you let into the New York Marathon as a special favor actually *won* the Boston Marathon?"

Like a thunderclap, I remembered. About a month before our marathon, after our entries were closed, this girl had come to me at the YMCA and said she knew about a woman who was terminally ill with a brain tumor, with not much time to live, and whose last wish was to run the New York City Marathon. Who was I to deny anybody's last wish? I had told her I needed two letters, one from the woman's doctor saying it was medically okay for her to run the marathon, and one from a lawyer saying she wouldn't sue us if anything went wrong. I got the letters and accepted her entry.

That small piece of the puzzle, at least, was in place.

Allan and I screened the videotape of the finish. Ruiz didn't appear at her recorded time, or anywhere near it, or anywhere at all among the finishers. Further, we talked to the woman who had finished two seconds ahead of Ruiz's time and the woman who had finished just after. Neither of them had seen any other woman close-by.

Ruiz had entered the marathon but had not finished. Major pieces were still missing. The media were all over me. The Rosie Ruiz story had instantly blossomed into a nationwide scandal (complete with Johnny Carson jokes). And I was getting angrier all the time. Having labeled her as a fraud, we were stuck with this damned awkward and paradoxical fact of having ourselves recorded her finish with our bar codes, and yet I had no explanation.

Two nights later I received a phone call from a guy who said his girl friend had some information about Rosie Ruiz, but she was very reluctant to tell anybody about it because it had become such a big, intimidating story. I convinced him to put her on the phone. She was Susan Morrow, a photographer, and she told me this story:

On her way to see the finish of the marathon she had boarded the subway in Greenwich Village just before noon. She saw a woman wearing running clothes, with a marathon number pinned on her shirt, and talked to her. The woman introduced herself as Rosie Ruiz and said she had dropped out of the race with an injury to her foot or ankle; she, too, was headed for the finish. They exchanged telephone numbers, with the idea that maybe they would get together sometime.

They got off the subway at Columbus Circle and walked to the finish-line area together. They walked around the bleachers, and Susan watched Rosie, still wearing her number, go through the barricades behind the finish line, into the chute area. Rosie told officials she had hurt her leg, and medical personnel immediately took her away to the first-aid area.

I could instantly deduce the rest of what happened there. The medics, as they are instructed in dealing with injured runners, took her directly for treatment without having her go through the chute. Assuming she was a finisher, they removed the bar code from her number and gave it to the scorers.

Before I could call a press conference to announce our discovery, Steve Marek and Rosie Ruiz held one of their own. I had never seen so much press in my life. It seemed like a hundred microphones were in front of them in the packed room at New York's Summit Hotel. Rosie appeared with her Boston Marathon medal draped around her neck and displayed her New York City Marathon finisher's certificate. Rosie called me, among other things, a liar. They announced that she would be running in other races soon.

I had Susan Morrow in discreet attendance to make sure of her identification: This Rosie Ruiz was the same woman she had met on the subway.

The next day I called a press conference at Tavern-on-the-Green, in Central Park, to announce our official disqualification of Ruiz and present our evidence.

Just before we began, Alice Cashman, from the Parks Department, came up to me with three messages. They were from Jack Rudin, of the Rudin family, our original sponsor; Parks Commissioner Davis; and Mayor Koch. All three messages implored me to cool it, lay off Rosie Ruiz—I was going too far. Other sponsors had called me to suggest I back off. Even my brother had called from Cleveland, advising me that it was in my best interests to shut up.

I wasn't trying to destroy Rosie Ruiz. I felt the overriding principle was restoration of our marathon's integrity. I presented Susan Morrow and the two women who finished around Ruiz's asserted time, and played the videotape for the press.

At the same time, Boston officials, having at long last determined through witnesses that Ruiz did not run their race either, but apparently jumped in just half a mile from the finish, disqualified her and bestowed the victory wreath on Jacqueline Gareau.

What got Ruiz to Boston in the first place was that, three months after our race, when she received our certificate, she showed it to her boss at the international metal-trading company where she worked. Himself a marathoner, her boss recognized how fine her finishing time was and rewarded her by paying her way to the Boston Marathon (she "ran" wearing her company's T-shirt).

My gut feeling is that Ruiz never intended to cheat in New York but that once she got her certificate (which probably surprised her because it was unlikely that she was familiar with our scoring system, for which her bar code was taken, and therefore wouldn't even have been aware that she was a "finisher"), she got caught up in the fairy tale and got in over her head. It turned out that she *had* once suffered from a brain tumor, which was removed and was benign; but that was seven years earlier, and apparently she had fully recovered.

If she intended to make any money on the Boston deal, she didn't. No magazine piece, no book, no movie. Maybe she could have made a buck by telling the whole story. But she never did come clean.

It was, finally, just a sad tale that upset a lot of people. The significant message it delivered to us was that the marathon game had become so big, so prominent, so newsworthy, so opulent in opportunity, that substantial fraud, even for financial gain, was a striking possibility.

The sport I had discovered as a little clique of runners in the Bronx in 1969 now needed standards and controls like any big-time professional sport to prevent big-time rip-offs. (We would begin by positioning videotape cameras at unrevealed places along the course for spotting purposes.)

Getting big and keeping control had become a kind of theme of the time—within our own house, the New York Road Runners Club.

From the onset of my presidency in 1972 I had run things pretty much on my own. For the first couple of years of the five-borough marathon things had been so wild and crazy that the club even forgot to hold elections. I didn't call meetings of the board of directors, didn't consult the officers, basically made all the important decisions myself. I didn't think about it. I was too busy directing and expanding our programs, advancing the marathon, to be bothered with our own bureaucracy. I did what I wanted to do. The marathon was successful. Our membership was growing. Our race calendar was getting filled. I changed our newsletter to a newspaper, then to a magazine. I instituted merchandising. Our promotion machinery was humming.

By 1978 there was another hum that I wasn't paying attention to, and that was one of discontent on the board of directors. I was getting public attention, and after a couple of years of my ignoring them, some of the board felt my wings should be clipped. I went away for about a month to Asia, on my last trip as a clothing consultant, and while I was gone, a bunch of board members decided I'd gone too far. When I came back, I found they had written up a new set of proposed bylaws that would severely restrict my power—the presidency would be a one-year term, any expenditure of more than one thousand dollars would have to be approved by the board, things like that, which would essentially strip me of power to make the kinds of decisions I was accustomed to making on my own.

We had a pretty hostile board meeting. Essentially, what some of them didn't like was that I made unilateral decisions. I screamed and yelled. I said that it looked like I wouldn't be president for another year, or if I was, I would be worthless because I couldn't make any decisions. I didn't threaten to quit, but I accused them of being petty and ungrateful, because the decisions I had made had turned out to be good for the club and the marathon.

I reminded them that I personally paid for much of the marathon in the beginning, and I brought in sponsorships. "The biggest crime I have committed," I said, "is that we have been successful."

The vote was close, but I managed to eke out a victory and maintain my power. At the same time, I knew I had to be more attentive to the board, to consult more often with them, keep them more abreast of my plans and maneuvers.

So that crisis had been laid to rest for the time, and we

proceeded to manage the external crises like wheelchairs and Rosie Ruiz and keep the marathon on track.

But under my nose another crisis was brewing, the last kind I would have expected, a much more personal and private one which threatened the 1980 marathon—a romantic triangle among my three most important people.

Allan Steinfeld and Alice Schneider had been living together since 1976. They were two of my favorite people, they were a terrific couple, and as far as work goes, they were a great team. We still had our main offices at the West Side Y, now overflowing eight or nine rooms. We had additional space, which we called our "secret office" (we didn't tell the public about it so that the people working there wouldn't be bothered, especially during marathon time), at 1860 Broadway, a few blocks away.

My office was at the Y. Allan and Alice worked in the Broadway office. In 1979 a volunteer we'll call Julie came aboard as an assistant in race organization and direction. Next thing I knew, in February 1980 Allan had split up with Alice and moved out of the apartment they shared. He was falling in love with Julie.

Alice—so quietly pleasant, intelligent and dedicated, one of the most popular people in the whole organization—was of course extremely dejected. I and others consoled her as best we could. Strangely, the three of them continued to work together, more or less. Alice couldn't stand the proximity, so we got her a work-space in a storage area a few floors above. Somehow, everybody managed to continue functioning.

In the summer Allan went back to Alice. That left Julie hurt. Everybody around the club started taking sides. Within our small staff things got messy. Conflicting loyalties led to intrigues that poisoned the atmosphere and interfered with the high-pressure work to prepare for the marathon.

I tried for a while to ignore it. I tried to keep my mind on the marathon and get everybody else to do the same. So long as they all did their work on the marathon, all this other stuff was just soap opera.

It didn't stop. Now Allan got reinvolved with Julie and was at the same time torn, wanting to hold on to Alice, and getting his head all screwed up because he's not a philanderer. Nobody was happy.

That plunged Alice into despair. I took her out for a long walk in Central Park, to impart whatever bits of wisdom I had, which weren't much. I had such admiration for how well she had borne up through all of this, and otherwise so much respect for Allan, that I could only hope this was just a final, passing cloud that would blow over and leave them together.

But while I tried to lift Alice's spirits, inside I was growing furious about the situation. The mood of the whole club was down, everybody was distracted. Last-minute marathon details were going unattended. I couldn't trust anybody to keep their minds on the task at hand.

Finally it was all over. Allan and Alice were a committed couple again. But I was fed up. The next morning I railed at them all: "How can you let your private lives mess up the most important thing in the world, which is the New York City Marathon! I won't permit it!"

We managed to pull together and shape up the marathon. And it was a great day, introducing a great new marathoner—Alberto Salazar. Salazar, who was one of the world's best 10,000-meter runners but who had never run a marathon, had entered under a "Predicted Time" of "2:10," which only a handful of marathoners had ever achieved, and publicly issued the brassy prediction that he would win. He did—in a time of 2:09:41, beating Mexico's Rodolfo Gomez by half a minute. (This broke Bill Rodgers' string of four straight victories; Billy was tripped and fell at the four-teen-mile mark and finished fifth.) Grete Waitz won her third straight and set her third straight world record in 2:25:41. Patti Catalano, from Boston, broke her own American record with 2:29:33.

We came away with a terrific job done. But how close we had come to breaking down. Reflecting on the staff and private lives and priorities, I recognized how fragile an operation such as ours is, when we have to rely on supreme concentration from a group of people who are underpaid—or unpaid—and overworked. By comparison with the triangle I had seen, my outside entanglements in romantic affairs seemed trivial; these people had gone at it with real seriousness. Romance is okay, even within the office. But I couldn't let such things intrude on the marathon.

8

For a long time, since before I got into running, I have tried to establish self-control, self-discipline, create an independence from external things so that nothing gets in the way of my work. Work has always been my highest priority. In any work I entered, I always wanted to get to the top. To maintain independence for pursuit of whatever I wanted to pursue, I didn't want to be saddled with needs for a fancy apartment or fancy clothes or expensive habits. I didn't want to be dependent on big meals or even regular meals because I wanted to stay lean and energetic, and I didn't want hunger to dictate my schedule. I didn't want to sleep too much, either, because that robbed me of hours. And I didn't want sex to get in the way.

When I was working in the Garment District, I felt a compulsion to eat: at least three meals a day, a lot of bread, and maybe three or four candy bars in between. I never got hugely overweight, but I did blow up to about 175, 20 pounds more than now. I embarked on a program of occasional fasting. First, it was just a total fast of twenty-four hours. Then I would extend it another twenty-four hours, taking just water or soft drinks. Off and on I would do that until I broke the dependence on food. Now I can often go without eating for half a day or a whole day without thinking about it—my appetite is more subservient to my schedule.

Similarly, years ago I was sleeping too much. I couldn't get up in the morning. I decided to do something about it. I would stay up late, until one in the morning, and force myself to get up at seven. Then I would stay up until two and still get up at seven. Gradually I shortened the hours until now and then I went to sleep at six and got up at seven. Sometimes I would experiment with sleeping as little as possible in four-night blocks. I might go totally without sleep for one night, then just sleep three hours the next, then maybe just two hours, and so on. Once in a while I even had "fake sleeps," which means I would stay up all night, then at quarter to seven I would set the alarm clock for seven, fall instantly asleep, wake up at seven, take a shower, and get dressed, pretending in my mind that I had slept all night. I would always go to work normally, convincing myself that I had had enough sleep. It changed things. I broke the psychological dependence on sleep to where four or five hours a night was plenty.

Even now, when I don't have to worry about getting fat because I run so much, and am accustomed to short nights of sleep, I still apply a little discipline as a habit: When I eat a meal, I will try to stop just a few bites before I feel satisfied; I will try to get out of bed when I feel I want just a few more winks.

With sex it was not a problem of overdoing it, just of letting it intrude at inopportune times. I allowed it to interfere with my business.

Near the end of my prerunning days I was flying to Hong Kong to meet with some important clothing buyers, and I got into conversation with a stewardess on the plane on which I was traveling. I mentioned another stewardess for that airline, named Sally, of whom I was very fond. I said I hadn't seen Sally in a long time and had lost track of her. I got off in Hong Kong, and the flight went on to Singapore.

That evening I got a call from Sally. She was in Singapore, waiting another day for a crew change, and this other stewardess had told her about meeting me. Sally was an exciting woman, and the coincidence of locating her was like a siren call which aroused me enough so that I took the next flight out that night for Singapore.

I would miss the meeting scheduled for the next morning with the buyers in Hong Kong, but I left a message saying I had been unavoidably detained. I figured the buyers would stick around, so I wouldn't lose anything. I was gone just long enough for one splendid night with Sally. When I got back to Hong Kong, the buyers were gone. They hadn't waited. They canceled our deal, and I lost a big chunk of business.

That wasn't the first time I had responded to an impromptu urge, but I had always been able to cover myself before. Now I had literally paid a steep price. I couldn't afford to allow momentary enchantment to interfere again with the task of the day. So I put a dramatic stop to it. I resolved to abstain totally from sex for a while. I didn't put any time limit on it, just for as long as it took me to get it firmly under control. I went for three months, then four months, and then figured I might as well make it half a year. I reached six months, and I was fine, not suffering, working hard. I was doing so well that I thought I hadn't yet put myself to a true test. I thought, let's try it for nine months. At nine months I thought, let's make it an even year. To make it even tougher on myself, I didn't stop dating, but in dating I stopped short of sex.

Finally, when the year was up, I found that it had been one of my most productive years ever as far as work was concerned. I had established my priorities and my ability to stick to them. I had greater confidence in my judgment to pick time and place for diversions—greater confidence in myself overall.

I've always been interested in social things, but whenever I got involved in a project, whether it was theater or the double-knit business or running, I became fanatically interested in it, wanted to master it completely. In the first few years of my involvement with running I immersed myself in it. There wasn't a magazine article or book published on running that I didn't read. I talked to every running coach or expert I could find. I spent more time on running than I ever had on other work.

My commitment to this priority didn't come cheap. Until I got into the running business I remained very close to my family in every respect. I have three brothers and a sister living in this country, and I used to see them often and participate in family events like holidays and birthdays. But when running took over, time was at a premium, and I had a choice to make. If I was to create a success with this world of running, fulfill the visions that I had, I had to make a sacrifice. I had to be very strong with myself and sacrifice family gatherings that I so very much enjoyed.

That made me a kind of black sheep of the family. Not only could I not spend time with my brothers and sisters, but I could not even devote the time to creating my own family. All my brothers and sisters got married. I have never completely given up the thought of having my own family, even now. Of the several close relationships I have had with women, maybe two or three of them could have developed into lasting relationships that included marriage and children. But that would have taken away from the time and energy I wanted to put into the world of running. The choice was mine, and the life-style I chose has its advantages.

Ten years ago a woman for whom I cared deeply left me because of my running (at least that was the expressed reason). I had gone with her for three and a half years. I'll call her Kate. I met her on a blind date, when she was about twenty-three and I was about forty. Kate was attending journalism school on her way to entering the publishing business. She was very studious and had no interest in running at all. Her tastes and interests were conservatively stylish. We both loved off-Broadway theater and concerts.

After we became quite attached, she sought a more traditional commitment from me and began giving me deadlines. First they were deadlines for getting married—I should make up my mind by April, then September. Then she gave up on that and would settle for living together—she just wanted a commitment of some kind. There was nothing unreasonable about it. I loved her. I don't know why I couldn't give her a commitment, except that

I've never been able to give one to anybody. Her deadlines always passed without confrontation.

Finally, in our third autumn, she said, "If we don't have a commitment by the end of this year, I'm leaving you."

I had recently become president of the NYRRC. I had been running a lot before, but when I became president I ran even more. I had to keep up my mileage to keep up with everybody else in the club. The most important thing in the world to me was to put in my mileage. I had become addicted. I would come home from work, spend time on club business, and then go running.

I kept a running diary, as most runners do, and logged in every day's run. That last year Kate and I were together, I had a goal of 2,500 miles for the year—it had been a New Year's resolution. I was obsessed with achieving that goal (runners will understand). Toward the end of the year I was getting close.

On New Year's Eve I spent the day flying back from the West Coast, where I had been on business. I had my running diary with me on the plane. I quickly totaled up my mileage for the year and found I was nineteen miles short.

That night we were going to a dinner party at an apartment on Central Park West, across town from Kate's apartment. I walked into her place about seven o'clock, coming straight from the airport. Kate had laid out my tuxedo and black tie and had my black shoes all polished. She was trying on the evening gown that she had bought especially for this party. She immediately grabbed me in a big hug. I had been gone a lot lately and hadn't been able to give her much affection. Nor was I responsive then. I told her I had checked my running diary and was nineteen miles short of my goal. "I don't have time for anything else before the party," I said. "I have to run."

She couldn't believe it. I couldn't really explain it, either, except to say rather lamely that I had to put in my mileage before the stroke of midnight or it wouldn't count for the year. I was completely out of touch with her feelings.

I went out for my run in Central Park. It was a dreary night, with a cold rain. It was a long run. I didn't dare quit right after nineteen miles because I was afraid I might have miscalculated in my diary. I ran another mile just to be sure. That took a couple of hours.

When I came back, she was sitting there in her evening gown, crying, her shoulders trembling. She wouldn't even look at me. I got dressed in a hurry. By the time I was ready, she had composed herself, reapplied her makeup, and seemed fine. We got to the party about ten, too late for dinner. But we danced and laughed and had a good time. At midnight we celebrated the new year with the other guests.

Then each of us danced with other guests, and I lost track of her. Later, when I looked for her, I couldn't find her. Somebody said she went home.

Home! Why would she do that? What could have happened? I telephoned, there was no answer.

I rushed out to get a taxi. It was impossible to find a taxi at 2 A.M. on New Year's Eve in the pouring rain. I had to walk—half running—about two miles to her place, through Central Park, and over to near the East River. Drenched and frozen, I was shaking with worry about her. I imagined all kinds of awful things. The only thing I didn't imagine was what really happened.

When I got there, my suitcase was in the hall outside her door. Next to it was a little bag with my running clothes in it. On the bag she had pinned an envelope with a note in it.

It was a long note, kind of summing up our relationship. She reminded me of her ultimatum, that if we didn't have a commitment by the end of the year she was leaving me. The year had ended a few hours ago. She added a P.S.: She had found my running diary, and just out of curiosity had added up the mileage. I had miscalculated, all right. Prior to New Year's Eve, I had run a total of 2,531 miles for the year—thirty-one miles over my goal. So I hadn't needed to run at all that night.

I didn't bother to knock on her door. I trudged the many weary blocks back to my own apartment, no longer noticing the rain or cold, carrying my suitcase and my little bag of running clothes.

For the next few weeks I tried to call her, but she would not speak with me. I sent her letters. They were returned unopened. When at last I started to get over the hurt, I began to realize that I was relieved, too, in a strange way. Although I missed her and what we had together, I really wasn't ready to make a commitment, and that difference between us had created a pressure that could not have been eased except by doing what she did.

Six months later she sent me a warm letter saying she had married, and was happy, and hoped everything was fine with me and my running. I was pleased for her, but I envied her happiness in a wistful way and for a time questioned whether my goals would bring me any similar contentment.

I didn't have another serious relationship for about five years. And then I fell in love harder than ever. Her name was Jennie. We didn't live together, but we traveled a lot and shared experiences while I roamed the world running in marathons and recruiting runners and absorbing ideas for developing our own.

In those days I was also running low on money. Although I was working full-time—more than full-time—for the club, I didn't take a salary because I felt the club couldn't afford it. I had been living on my savings from the garment business, and the savings were dwindling. At Jennie's insistence we starting going out dutch. At about the same time, I launched our "Run to Work" movement, urging busy people to forgo taxis and public transportation and commute by running instead, using the time to shape up. It was a convenient and practical movement for me because I wanted to save money. I saved money on transportation *and* clothes because, to set an example, I took to wearing running clothes everywhere I went. And I ran everywhere. I got quite a bit of publicity for the movement because I showed up at important meetings and fancy restaurants wearing running clothes. When the transit strike hit New York in 1980, the movement got a big boost.

Looking back, I can imagine that having to go dutch all the time and with a guy who was always in running clothes and always running, wore a little thin with Jennie. She tried running herself, to share it with me, but her heart wasn't in it, and she didn't really care for the whole running scene.

In the spring of 1981, six months before the marathon, I had gone to Madrid to observe the World Cross Country Championships, and Jennie was supposed to meet me in Paris afterward. But she never showed up. She had decided to break up with me.

After one serious parting I started running a marathon every month, a regimen I never supposed I could maintain, but have maintained right up to the present day. I have accomplished far more than ever before. Maybe a wrenching loss forces you to reach down deep for strengths you didn't know you had. Who knows? I don't try to analyze it much. I'm mellower now.

And after years of long hours, seven-day workweeks, unpredictable schedules, I've gotten used to not being able to plan for social things, to not being able to devote myself consistently to developing a relationship. So far, my priorities remain those for which I opted long ago. As for social life, I have to take it pretty much as it comes.

If being known as the director of the marathon provides opportunities, so does *knowing* the director of the marathon. Since it is now so difficult to get into the race, people try all kinds of ploys, bribes, and pressures in attempts to use me to get them in. There have been several incidents of women engaging in flirtation in an attempt to get marathon entry.

A woman called from Massachusetts to tell me she had received a rejection notice from the marathon and wanted to come to New York to talk to me about it.

She came to my office. She was about thirty, tall, blond, not athletic-looking. She told me she had never run a marathon before. Her husband had recently left her, and she started running as a kind of therapy. And now, running a marathon had become the most important thing in her life—especially the New York City Marathon because it was the biggest and most widely publicized. She had to prove to herself, and to her former husband, that she was worth something, that she could accomplish something so challenging on her own. We talked about that awhile, and she told me how sympathetic and kind I was to listen. And then she started telling me how much she liked me. She said she would like to spend some time with me in New York.

I said, "Do you really like me, or do you just want to be accepted for the marathon?"

She lowered her eyes and said, "I do like you, but the truth is I want to be accepted."

I liked her, too, for her honesty. And she was very attractive. I was going through a lonely period, and I was tempted to pursue her interest in me, real or not. But I didn't. I did, though, pass on her request to the Appeals Committee. I believed her story and I appreciated her reasons for wanting to run.

A year or so later I ran into her in New York. I asked her out. She declined. She said, "You're really not my type."

A more crude attempt came from a petite actress who joined us as a volunteer for the marathon. This was one of the years when we used the former Huntington Hartford Museum as marathon headquarters. It was just two or three days before the marathon, when things were frantic, and I was at one of the night meetings of the volunteer staff on the tenth floor. It was very warm, and I slipped out of the meeting to get some air on the balcony. She followed me. In the dark we got into quiet conversation, standing very close.

She said her husband had run the marathon previously but had been rejected this year. She had joined up as a volunteer, she said, in hopes that would help us change our mind about accepting her husband. I was noncommital. I wasn't in the mood to debate it. She got very direct. She said she wanted her husband accepted and would do whatever was necessary to make that happen. At the same time, she pressed up against me and started caressing me all over.

I rejected her advances, and her husband stayed rejected, too. She didn't serve as a volunteer, and I never saw her again.

The sexual game to get into the marathon also happens in the reverse. One of our female employees was suddenly swept off her feet by a guy who came on like Prince Charming. He showed her every affection and attention, took her to the best places, appeared for all the world to have the most serious intentions about her. Until marathon time came along. And then he wanted her to get him into the race. When she said she couldn't, that he would have to go through the regular procedures, he dropped her cold.

Obviously, with so many people wanting like crazy to get into the marathon (people have hawked marathon numbers outside our hotel headquarters for prices as high as $100), there is considerable potential for abuse in my position. I have never taken a bribe, but I've been offered plenty. It is reasonably common for offers to come to me or other senior officials of our club in amounts of $500, $1,000, or $2,000.

A few years ago a contractor we'd used for some work tried to give me $1,000 in cash. He assumed a kickback was part of the deal—that's the way it works in this city, he said. He also assumed that part of the deal included that his son would get into the marathon. I told him: No deal, and no more work for you.

In 1981 a guy came to see me with the crazy idea of raffling off a house in a race he wanted to put on. He offered me $1,000 to endorse the race. When I said no, he offered $2,000, then $3,000, until finally he understood that my "no" meant "no" at any price.

One time a major Wall Street brokerage firm contacted me to say they wanted to become a sponsor of the marathon. At the same time, they said they wanted a dozen entries for top company officers. I told them I couldn't accept their sponsorship. It's one thing to become a sponsor and then ask us to consider granting a couple of entries to key people we work with. But nobody can make entries a part of the arrangement to become a sponsor.

I would like to think that word has pretty much got around by now that bribes don't work. But even in 1983 one of our officers told me a man had offered him $5,000 for an entry. A Wall Street bond salesman offered $500.

The one sure way of not getting accepted for our marathon is to offer a bribe. Once you've offered a bribe, you'll be rejected, no matter what.

Actually, when it comes close to marathon time, I'm pretty oblivious to any kind of advances—sexual, financial, whatever.

The marathon is so all-consuming that the rest of my life is shut out.

I do my best to remain oblivious to everything except our preparations for Marathon Sunday. Nothing can be allowed to compromise the New York City Marathon. That same attitude pervades our staff. That's why we've been able to make it work.

9

Nineteen eighty-one was a year that turned out to be almost too good. Sometimes I wondered whether we could ever top it or measure up to it, whether we had peaked and everything afterward would be anticlimactic. In the spring we moved into our new building. In September we put on the first 5th Avenue Mile. And in October we saw double world records set in the marathon before a national network television audience.

Buying our building, the International Running Center, was a coup. Two years before, when it became apparent that we needed more space and the West Side YMCA needed the space we already had for other purposes, we had no money. Larger quarters somewhere else would cost considerably more in rent, and we were already operating at a deficit. We faced the paradox of not being able to afford rent and therefore having to buy—because to buy, we could have a fund-raising drive! We launched a drive led by Carl Landegger, board chairman of the Parsons & Whittemore paper-plant manufacturing company. A runner himself, Landegger was brought into our quest by our treasurer, Peter Roth, to lend his executive talents and contacts to our search for a new home.

In two years we raised enough from solicitations—through Landegger's operation, our mailings to members, and utilization of any and all contacts any of us had—to indicate that we might be able to afford a $600,000 building if we were lucky with the banks. A search committee spearheaded by Dick Traum, whose firm, Personnelmetrics, then handled our computer scoring, looked at more than fifty buildings all over Manhattan. Finally, they found this building at 9 East 89th Street. The first time I went to see it, we couldn't even get in. It was locked up tight, with no one on the premises. I liked the outside—classic, sturdy, stately. I loved the location—a great neighborhood near the Guggenheim Museum, Fifth Avenue, and Central Park. As I peered through the wrought-iron grillwork covering the glass doors, into the lobby, I said, "This is it, this is the one I want."

The price was $1,373,000, an impossible amount. I went to Manufacturers Hanover Trust, one of the marathon's primary sponsors, to see about a $1-million loan. The loan officer asked to see our annual report. The report showed a deficit. The officer asked a fair question: How could the bank lend a million dollars to such an organization? But he picked up the phone and called a superior official, described our request, hung up the phone, and said we had the loan. I don't know what magic was worked. Along with such a demonstration of faith and trust by the bank, ten of our prominent members cosigned for the loan, and a dozen other corporations and foundations chipped in.

As a result of such great faith in our potential, we now had the biggest headquarters of any running organization in the world.

The next to show great faith was network television—finally. I had been trying to get the networks interested in live coverage of the marathon since 1976. CBS thought there was no way you could televise a marathon successfully on Sunday morning, but perhaps if it were Sunday afternoon I might attract local coverage. NBC thought it could be done on a Saturday afternoon, fitting it in during half-time and time-outs of a football game.

As anxious as I was to get the marathon on the air I wasn't going to compromise it, even to get network television. I wouldn't start the marathon at midday because there is still a chance of hot weather in October—we have had temperatures in the 80s—and I wouldn't start runners in the heat of midday. I wouldn't start in midafternoon, either, because the last runners would be finishing in the dark.

In 1977 we got a little coverage of the start and finish from an obscure cable channel (cable was then in its infancy, watched by hardly anyone). In 1978 CBS gave us a couple minutes of taped coverage on Sunday afternoon. In 1979 and 1980 Alan Lubell's Marathon Entertainment produced live coverage to syndicated stations, but there were extensive technical problems both years, and it didn't work well. I give them credit for breaking the barrier to put us on live.

From this experience I was more convinced than ever that we had to have network coverage and that once I could lure in a network, the ratings would back us up.

ABC was the first network that seemed to understand what I was talking about and to show real interest. I met with ABC's Bob Iger (himself a runner), who buys sports programs for ABC-TV, early in 1980. His interest had already been aroused by the possibilities he saw from the syndicated coverage, shown in New York on Channel 5. Ultimately, he thought, the marathon could be big enough to join the ranks of such television sports spectaculars as the Kentucky Derby, the World Series, and the Super Bowl. And he agreed that it must be live.

Aside from the cost, Iger's main concerns were how to sustain audience interest for two and a half hours (CBS and NBC had figured that only the start and finish were exciting; the middle was boring) and how to guarantee exclusivity of coverage on the public streets of the city. I wasn't worried about the audience; I was confident it would be there and stay there. The Kentucky Derby, a two-minute race, gets an hour and a half of coverage— almost all of it vignettes and interviews. The marathon, on the other hand, is a race the entire two and a half hours, with lead changes, ploys, dramas, the whole time.

Naturally, if ABC was to commit itself to live coverage, they had to be guaranteed exclusivity. The marathon is run on public property, so theoretically we couldn't guarantee "rights to the streets." We have no absolute right to prohibit somebody from just holding up a camera in the crowd somewhere along the course. But in practical fact the city gives us control over the conduct of the marathon, including placements of press trucks and buses and who rides in them, and press positions at the start and finish. Though there may be no precedent for it, the city has actually put us in charge of issuing the official permits for those positions. So if any members of the press want a preferential position, unhampered by the crowd and the police, they must receive a permit from us. With that practicality in mind we could guarantee our exclusive cooperation for television to ABC and thus guarantee exclusivity.

When we began actual negotiations in September of 1980, I didn't care how much money we were going to get. I let the lawyers do the talking. But in the back of my mind I didn't give a damn whether ABC paid us $5,000, or even if we had to *pay* ABC $5,000—I just wanted to get us on the network. I was sure the ratings would surpass what they expected. After all, logic told me that if a golf match—to me one of the most boring games in sport—receives high enough ratings to justify network coverage, all we needed to show was a good duel of top runners in Brooklyn, on First Avenue, in Central Park, and that would be more exciting than the most exciting of golf matches. So if we didn't make any money the first year, or even the second, I was sure we would more than make it up eventually.

We signed a four-year contract in June 1981 to run through the 1984 marathon. A confidentiality clause in the contract prohibited me from revealing details. I let the press speculate on what we got, and guesses went as high as $1 million a year. What we actually got was, by network standards, laughably low, a very small percentage of what was speculated. I figured that by 1985 we would be able to demand a fee justifying the speculation.

Now with our own building, and the first-ever live network television contract for a marathon outside of the Olympics, we came up with another first: the 5th Avenue Mile. Putting a mile run down the plushest residential section of New York's plushest avenue was an idea as outrageous as it was enticing. First of all, the mile run is a track event, not a road event, always on an oval track indoors or outdoors. Second, we are a road-running club, not a track club, and top milers are in a world apart from top marathoners. Third, Fifth Avenue is the scene of most of the city's major parades, so many of them that the merchants and residents have protested sternly against any further extraordinary use of their street. So it was a great idea.

It came to me when I attended the 1980 Millrose Games, the country's most prestigious indoor track and field meet, in Madison Square Garden. The mile is the centerpiece of those games, and it is treated with high drama. They cut the lights, the announcer intones, "Ladies and gentlemen, the Wanamaker Mile." And then the lights come on and the crowd goes crazy and the world's top milers go to the line for the most famous mile run in the world. It was the most emotional and exciting moment I had experienced in the world of track and field. World-indoor-record holder Eamonn Coghlan, an Irishman now a resident of a New York suburb, won that mile.

At a reception afterward I congratulated Coghlan and said, "Isn't it a shame that only eighteen thousand people were there to see you win such a magnificent event? Maybe we should get you and the others out on Fifth Avenue to run in front of a hundred thousand people."

He took it as a serious suggestion, later reminded me of it, so I decided to push it. It would be organized and directed by Allan Steinfeld, who knew much more about the mile and milers than I did.

We thought it could be a spectacular event for the early autumn, using Fifth Avenue from the Metropolitan Museum of Art, at 82nd Street, down to 62nd Street. On the right side of the runners would be Central Park, with the wide sidewalk where we could put up bleachers; on their left would be the avenue's most elegant apartment buildings. What a sight for television—the world's top milers, framed by that scenery, dashing down the middle of Fifth Avenue!

Most of the people I talked to about it thought I was crazy. There was no way the city would let me do it. And even if the city did permit it, we wouldn't get anything like the 100,000 spectators I was talking about—let alone television—or even any top runners because it would be on a road, not a track, and would never enter record books as an official "mile."

That made it all the more challenging to us. There ensued the most nerve-wracking roller-coaster ride of ups and downs, approvals and disapprovals, I had ever experienced.

We picked the date of September 26. Parks Commissioner Gordon Davis said that before his department would approve it, we had to get approval from the residents themselves, a Fifth Avenue Community Board.

I made the presentation to the Community Board, thirty-four staid people, most of them women, all of whom seemed to regard me initially as something from another planet. The first reactions were negative. I dug in and pitched harder. I told them that just as Fifth Avenue is the most charismatic street, the mile is the most charismatic event of track and field, that unlike a parade with a beer-drinking crowd that leaves filth in its wake, this would be a prestigious event with an elegant crowd befitting the neighborhood, that the mile would tie up the street for only a short time, that we were, after all, the people who put on the marathon, the most successful and efficient of all city-wide events. I begged them to give us a chance.

People started to speak in support. The vote was 32–2 in favor.

Armed with that approval, I went to the Police Department. They turned us down. Too many of their personnel were committed to security for a rugby match involving a controversial South African team, which was scheduled for the same date. I appealed to Parks Commissioner Davis, who by then was in full support, and he interceded and convinced the P.D. to reverse their decision.

In the summer we went to Oslo, where most of the world's top milers were gathered for the Oslo Dream Mile. They all loved the idea, including Steve Ovett, the Englishman who won the Dream Mile and then set the world record in Germany.

Having landed ABC-TV for the marathon, I now sold them the 5th Avenue Mile. It was an easy sale because we had Ovett. ABC scheduled it for *Wide World of Sports*. We hyped it further with a print advertising campaign that headlined "Ovett at the Met" (the starting line being at the Metropolitan Museum of Art).

We needed a sponsor because of our high start-up cost, in addition to bringing in twenty-six elite runners (thirteen men, thirteen women) from eight countries, which meant travel and hotel expenses, plus considerable appearance and incentive fees. Dangling ABC network coverage before their eyes, we got the Pepsi company to sponsor it for $175,000, in exchange for which we agreed to call the event the Pepsi Challenge 5th Avenue Mile (the only time we let a sponsor attach its name).

Then everything started to come apart. A month before the mile I was in Stockholm to run the Stockholm Marathon and do some negotiating for our marathon. I got a frantic call from our office in New York: The Police Department had suddenly canceled the 5th Avenue Mile. One of the newspapers had inadvertently printed that we expected a crowd of 1 million—instead of the correct 100,000—and the P.D. wasn't going to control a million people for us. I took the first plane back to New York.

Even though it had been a mistake, the P.D. had by then notified all departments concerned that the event was off, and now they wouldn't reverse themselves. It was the toughest political struggle I had ever had in New York. I had to use all my contacts, cash in all my IOUs, take the case all the way to the mayor's office, to finally get the event reinstated.

No sooner had I accomplished that than the IAAF, the world governing body, got into the act. President Adriaan Paulen, an elderly Dutchman, told the press at an IAAF meeting in Sarajevo, Yugoslavia, that the 5th Avenue Mile represented gross commercialism and would not receive an international sanction; any athlete who took part would jeopardize his or her amateur status.

Immediately, we started getting cancellations from athletes. The whole deal was going down the tube. I couldn't reach Paulen by telephone, so I flew to Rome, where he was due for another meeting. I met him in the lobby of his hotel and tried to reason with him. I even presented him with a silver apple as a token of New York City. He was immovable. He treated the 5th Avenue Mile as a bad joke.

By the greatest of luck his term was just then coming to an end. A couple of days later he was replaced as president by Primo Nebiolo, of Italy. With the helpful intervention of several other interested parties, I was able to swing Nebiolo to our side. He saw the 5th Avenue Mile, including Ovett and the fastest field of milers ever assembled, as a great promotion for track and field.

We were back in business. But then Ovett suddenly canceled, due to illness.

Our deal with ABC—and by implication everybody else—had hinged on the presence of Ovett. For a brief time ABC quivered with doubt, but finally, to their credit, the network held firm on the deal, recognizing that even without Ovett we still had a most remarkable group of milers in a remarkable event.

A crowd estimated by police at more than 100,000 and a national TV audience watched Sidney Maree, a South African attending Villanova University, win the men's mile and Leann Warren, of the University of Oregon, win the women's. The event was instantly established as an annual celebrated race and quickly spawned an international circuit of city-street miles—in Rome, Paris, Dublin, Rio de Janeiro, Toronto (Tokyo, Moscow, and London are laying the groundwork for joining the circuit). It was one of our proudest accomplishments—and one of the most dramatic examples of Allan's expertise and efficiency.

We were now on the threshold of our crowning event of the year, in which 2.5 million spectators and 12 million television viewers would witness a man and a woman achieve world records in the same marathon.

Those in New York had already seen three world records for women, all by Grete Waitz, the latest a 2:25:41 in our previous marathon. But the men's record of 2:08:34, set by Australia's Derek Clayton, in Antwerp, Belgium, had stood for twelve years. Nobody else had even run under 2:09. Alberto Salazar, who had brashly predicted victory in his first marathon in 1980, and won in 2:09:41, was brash again in 1981. Not only did he expect to win, but he said he was stronger and faster than the year before, and a world record was a possibility. To knock a minute off his time was a tall order, but Salazar had come on the scene so amazingly fast that nobody knew *what* he might be capable of. He was the first of a new breed that would transform the marathon by combining speed with traditional marathon endurance.

Whether his first marathon victory—and his only marathon to date—had been a fluke or not was hard to tell. He put a lot of pressure on himself with his confident—though not cocky—predictions. He would be well tested by a field that included Tony Sandoval, who had won the U.S. Olympic trials in Buffalo in 1980 (the year we boycotted the Moscow Olympics), and Mexico's Rodolfo Gomez, who had finished second to Salazar last year. Bill Rodgers was planning to run, too (this was the year when he got fed up with sponsors at the last minute and withdrew).

Grete Waitz was not predicting a world record or even a victory—she never does. But this year she wasn't even sure she could run. Two weeks before the marathon she had come down with a severe case of shin splints. She called from Oslo to tell us about the problem and ask if we still wanted her under the circumstances. I definitely wanted her, and we recommended an excellent doctor.

This year we were hyping the prospects for the most dramatic showdown ever in the women' race. In April, Allison Roe, of New Zealand, a statuesque, twenty-five-year-old blonde, had won the Boston Marathon with the second fastest time ever in the world, 2:26:46, a little more than a minute off Grete's record. Grete had always won easily, but she had never raced against Allison Roe, and with Roe there to push her this year we expected real fireworks.

Even Roe's presence was in doubt until just before the marathon. She had participated for open prize money at the Cascade Run Off in Portland, Oregon, in June, part of the unsanctioned open circuit set up by the Association of Road Racing Athletes, which was challenging the international amateur policies. (Participation at Cascade would keep American-record holder Patti Catalano out of our 1981 race.) The New Zealand Amateur Athletic Association banned Roe from sanctioned competition, but she turned over her $4,000 winnings from Cascade to her association and appealed the ban. The world governing body, IAAF, was even then trying to come up with a formula for trust funds that would allow athletes to be paid.

For weeks I tried to get clarification of her status from the New Zealand association. In early October she notified us that her ban had been lifted. But Ollan Cassell, executive director of the U.S. association, TAC, insisted she was still banned. It wasn't cleared up until ten days before our marathon.

Grete Waitz spent the pre-race week in New York, getting all kinds of medical treatments for her legs and running a little to test herself. By race morning she still didn't know how far or how fast she could run.

From the start of the race it was clear that the lead pack of the men's field was keying on Salazar, running his pace. For several miles two dozen men clustered around him. By the halfway point there were four, and the split was 1:04:10, a world-record pace. But we had seen world-record paces at that point before; it was too early to tell. On First Avenue in Manhattan it was just Salazar and Mexico's José Gómez (no relation to Rodolfo). Suddenly, in the seventeenth mile Salazar surged away from Gómez with an incredible 4:33 for that mile.

With that, I said to Charlie McCabe, of Manufacturers Hanover (who always rides in the lead car with me), "It might be a world record."

"We might have a double world record," Charlie said, noting that the progress in the women's race, which we tracked by radio, had a record pace also.

"There's as much chance of that," I said, "as of me turning into a woman."

Julie Brown, of San Diego, a former Olympian who had once held the American record, was leading, with Roe and Waitz right behind her. But at fifteen miles Grete had to drop out with her leg problems. I didn't think Julie could maintain the pace; and without Grete to push her I didn't think Allison Roe could hold it either.

Meanwhile, Salazar, all by himself, continued clicking off hot miles. When we turned into Central Park at Columbus Circle, it looked like he could do it. The 75,000 spectators there knew about the possibility, too, from the P.A. announcer, and were roaring in anticipation. We sped to the finish line, where I leaped out of the car and ran to the banner. Alberto came into view a few hundred yards away. It was clear he would smash the record. At 2:08:13 he swept across under the banner and sagged into the arms of finish-line officials. He had beaten the twelve-year-old record by twenty-one seconds.

The crowd noise didn't stop. I was too occupied with Salazar to hear the P.A. announcer advise the crowd that Allison Roe, too, was on a world-record pace and that they should greet her entrance into the park and urge her on with their cheers. So I wasn't in my usual place out on the course to guide her in under the banner. She finished in 2:25:29, twelve seconds under Grete Waitz's year-old record—four and a half minutes ahead of the next woman, Grete's countrywoman Ingrid Kristiansen.

(It was not totally academic whether I guided Allison in. The finish-line banner has sponsors' names spread across it. Our agreement is that, for publicity purposes, the first man finishes under "Perrier" and the first woman under "Manufacturers Hanover." I took some flak from the bank for my lapse, which allowed Allison Roe, like Salazar, to finish under "Perrier.")

It was truly my greatest day ever—the greatest day for the club and for the marathon. The dream of dreams had been to have world records for both men and women occur in the same race in front of network TV cameras.

I suffered my usual postmarathon depression afterward, but it was worse this time. Instead of a day or two, it lasted many days, and it was deeper. Not only did I have no one to share my greatest day with (because of my recent romantic breakup), but it had also been too complete, too quick a fulfillment of my fantasies. Suddenly, I didn't know what was left to accomplish. It was a little frightening to think of what might come next—or what might not come.

But the reality is that world records come and go. There was still work to do to improve the total marathon, the "people's marathon" for all the runners—that was still the foundation. As for the world records and elite runners, competition was now so deep around the world that there were bound to be new stars, new excitement, big surprises coming up. After a time I regained control of my head, restored my optimism, and went back to work with renewed spirit.

Since 1977 I had been trying to get Russian runners. The Russians had never participated in a road race in the United States, even though in 1978 they had the top-rated marathoner in the world, Leonid Moseyev (Moseyev and I became friendly over the years; he liked to wear the New York City Marathon cap I gave him). Officially, if you want a foreign runner, you make the request through your governing body to theirs. But if you do that with the Iron Curtain countries, nine out of ten times you won't get any athletes. Every year we sent invitations through TAC to the Russian federation; every year they regretfully declined.

In other Eastern European countries I was moderately successful by making personal contact. In those days road racing was still treated like the bastard offspring of track and field, and our relationship with TAC was strained; TAC kept us at arm's length, ignored us at meetings. Foreign federations, too, were used to dealing with track and field, and they didn't know quite how to handle road racing. So especially with Eastern European countries, which were naturally more suspicious of official contacts with the United States, I went out of my way to deal with them on a personal basis. Most of the time I wouldn't even tell TAC I was going to those countries. I would go as a private citizen.

In Russia and the People's Republic of China that is all you can do—try to make personal contact that breaks the ice. In some other countries you can go a little further.

Coming from Rumania, I knew that even to get an official copy of a birth certificate you had to use influence, do favors. In all of Eastern Europe, officials at all levels have low salaries and are receptive to favors. And so, in discreet ways, you try to make personal contact with the right people, officials with influence, and help them out, make them kindly disposed on a personal level.

In dealing for runners it can be quite an indirect thing—a variation of the common American college practice of recruiting athletes by wining and dining influential people around them, creating personal relationships. I just tried to allow my experience and instincts to be my guide.

I went to Poland a few years ago to make a presentation to the federation in Warsaw to try to get athletes. I had some friends there who spoke good English. One of them and a federation official and I went for a walk to talk about my interests in athletes. It was winter, very cold. I wanted to buy another sweater. My friend took us to a private house where I could get a much better deal than in a store, a kind of black-market place. I bought a sweater. I could see that this federation official was dying to get something for himself. I suggested that he try on a coat he liked. He said he couldn't afford it. I told him not to worry about it, I would help. That seemed to create a bond between us. From then on we have been able to get Polish runners for our marathon.

In Hungary it was easier, because I speak the language. After a few drinks with a key official in Budapest, and a friendly exchange, he promised us runners, and we got them.

It didn't work that way in East Germany. I got taken. East Germany has so far been an unsuccessful foreign venture. We've been inviting the Olympic champion, Waldemar Cierpinski, ever since he won the gold medal in Montreal in 1976 (he won the gold again in Moscow in 1980). I met Cierpinski once in Fukuoka, Japan. I speak enough German so that we could converse privately, without an interpreter. He said he'd like nothing more than to run the New York City Marathon. He even has a poster of our marathon displayed in his home. But it's not his decision. It's his federation's decision, and the East German federation always says no.

I wondered what the key to the East Germans was. A friend of mine, an American with a lot of international experience, said I was going about it wrong. With the East Germans, he said, you have to use special financial influence. Simply put: Give the right guy a thousand dollars, and they'll come.

I thought maybe he was right, maybe I was being too proper with them. On a subsequent trip there I was guided to an East German who let on that he was the one in charge of deciding which runners go where. He said he would like to consider our marathon. Against my better instincts, I gave him five hundred dollars. He gave me the clear impression that the amount was sufficient, that he would grant our request for runners. I should have recognized that not only was it wrong, it was all too easy. We didn't get any East German runners. Many months later I found out that this guy was merely an unimportant clerk who didn't even work for the federation, just a hanger-on who liked to brag. Naturally, I haven't tried the misguided direct financial approach again.

In 1979 we got three runners from China, mediocre ones. But none since. In 1983 I met with the Chinese federation in Peking. They said they would not send us any men because they now have the men's marathon in Peking just a month before ours. And they couldn't send us any women, they said, because they were going to send the women to a "Hollywood" marathon in November.

I was very curious about that because I had never heard of it, so I talked to the head of the Chinese women's federation. She affirmed that they had already committed their women to a "very important marathon" in Los Angeles. She said President Reagan was going to be the official starter of that race and that it was being put on by "the director of the Boston Marathon," Marshall Medoff.

I could only laugh. Marshall Medoff, the guy who got into heavy litigation over the Boston Marathon, was reported to have promoted the idea of this Hollywood marathon to the Chinese. And the Chinese federation couldn't send any women to New York because of that. I didn't argue, but I doubted anything would come of the Hollywood marathon, and it didn't.

But the ones I really wanted were the Russians. And I really went after them for 1982.

For a number of years I had been meeting the Russians at various international competitions. They would send runners to the European championships and to Fukuoka, but not the United States. I became friendly with coaches and athletes. The Russians always greeted me very warmly. One year they gave me a samovar. I gave them T-shirts, of course. Every time I met them I urged them to come to New York. Every year they said they would love to come, but the Soviet federation made its decisions based on whatever priorities it had.

In 1981 they held the first Moscow Marathon. They expressed an interest in having somebody tell them more about road racing in America. In August 1982 I decided to go to the second Moscow Marathon. Ollan Cassell, the TAC executive director, set me up with an introduction to their federation.

I met with the federation in Moscow and presented them with literature about our marathon and T-shirts. And I took a copy of the film of our 1981 marathon (our official film is produced each year by Salmini Films). They were interested in the growth of the running movement in the United States, particularly so far as women are concerned; Russian women were great at shorter distances but far behind our marathon runners. We spent quite a bit of time talking.

Finally, my years of persistence were rewarded: They promised to send Russian athletes to our 1982 marathon.

I didn't trust them to follow through. A month later, in September, I met them in Athens at the European Championships. At a reception for international organizations I met a Greek woman who was the official interpreter at the championships. She was gorgeous, and when I found out that she spoke fluent Russian, I grabbed her arm and took her directly over to the head of the Russian delegation. I wanted her to impress this Russian official with the importance of the New York City Marathon and to remind him of their promise in Moscow to send me runners. I asked her to be especially friendly to him because I had worked so hard to get their attention.

The Russian official loved her. She became my interpreter for the evening. And when the evening was over, the Russian told me, through her interpretation, that our film of the 1981 marathon had impressed them tremendously and that they were convinced it was in their best interest to send the runners to New York. And even if our presentation hadn't worked, he added, how could he resist the urging of such a beautiful woman?

We didn't put out much publicity about the Russians accepting our invitation, because until I saw them here in person, I still didn't believe they were going to come. But sure enough, they came, a team of three mediocre men and three of their best women. But by the time they arrived, just two days before the marathon, there wasn't much time to hype anything. Instead of sending the interpreter I had supposed was coming, the Russian journalist I had met in Moscow, they sent us a woman who spoke English haltingly, and didn't know much about the sport. Plus another man who didn't speak English at all, supposedly one of their coaches—but he seemed to know nothing whatsoever about the sport, and I suspected he was a security agent.

On Saturday, the day before the marathon, we held a press conference to announce the Russians, but it was a disaster. We had so many top runners from so many countries that the press was not very interested in Russians they had never heard of. And also, the interpreter's Engish was so lousy and her knowledge of the sport so slight that we spent most of the time trying to explain to her what the questions were about and trying to understand her obscure answers. (Ultimately, one of the Russian women, Nadezhda Gumerova, did run very well, finishing eighth and setting a Russian women's record with a time of 2:35:28.)

We were almost able to give open prize money in 1982. After years of haggling among athletes and officials about amateurism, Olympic eligibility, under-the-table payments, and competition from Eastern European athletes who are state-supported, in the spring of 1982 TAC finally came up with an acceptable formula to allow U.S. athletes to receive prize money without losing their eligibility for the Olympics: All money awarded to athletes would go into individual trust accounts administered by TAC. The athletes could withdraw the money for training or other expenses connected with the sport, which in practice meant just about anything at all—buying a car or a house, paying for school, going on holidays, etc. In September I attended the IAAF meeting in Athens, where the world governing body adopted the trust-fund idea for all its 170 member nations.

At last we in New York would be able to pay open prize money without engaging in cat-and-mouse games with the press and continuing the hypocrisy of under-the-table payments. Immediately, several marathons, including Chicago, went to an open-prize-money structure (Chicago announced $82,000 in total prize money). I even started telling the press off the record that we would probably award between $100,000 and $150,000 in open prize money.

But in October Mayor Koch vetoed the idea. He was worried about appearances of commercialism and wanted to wait and see how the plan worked in other places.

So once again in 1982—for what I hoped would be the last time—we had to keep our prize money under the table. TAC sanctioned our marathon without insisting that we file a prize-money list.

Just before the 1982 marathon we got into television trouble. Because there was a pro-football strike on, CBS was trying to find substitute sports for Sunday afternoon, and they asked me for permission to have a camera position at the finish line for a minute of live coverage.

Terrific, I thought, we get additional exposure. Just one minute of CBS news coverage right at the finish wouldn't infringe on ABC's territory. I granted permission.

Two days before the marathon Bob Iger, of ABC, got wind of it and was furious. I explained that it was just one minute of news and that other stations had cameras at the finish, too. He said it was *not* news, it was *CBS Sports* that was planning to do it— direct competition—and CBS was going *live,* whereas the other stations would use just one minute of *taped* coverage for later showing on their news editions. "It's a violation of our agreement!" he railed at me.

Deep into the next two nights, Friday and Saturday, we had heated and tense telephone negotiations that included Iger, Allan Steinfeld, the lawyers, and me. We went back and forth until 2 or 3 A.M. both nights. ABC couldn't stop CBS from televising the finish, because the permissions were up to us. But finally I was convinced that it would indeed violate our agreement for exclusive coverage. I had been completely naive, assuming it would be a CBS news item and that CBS would restrict their coverage to one minute. After all, their *NFL Today* show went on at 12:30, but they had no NFL games to preview. Timing was perfect to cover the finish. Once they got their cameras set up there at the finish line, what was to keep them from perhaps including taped highlights from the start and making an entire half-hour show out of it? I realized how dumb I had been in not grasping the possibilities, even though they were only that.

Now I was in a real bind. Having okayed the deal with CBS, I would now have to backtrack and withdraw the permission. I hated to seem like a fool or an unreliable bargainer to CBS. Who knows when we might want them for an event? What if after our ABC contract ran out, CBS might want to get into the bidding on the next one?

But I had no choice. I told CBS the deal was off.

But now my suspicious instincts were alert. Even with permission canceled, CBS had already made their plans, and what if a crew showed up? There was a place at the finish line where they had planned to put their camera, the only place they could do it, and it was on public property. Once a camera position was established there, we would have no time to move them out, and it could develop into a real hassle. Supposedly they wouldn't show up. But I couldn't count on that. I had to take some preemptive action. On Saturday morning I went to the finish line and had our workers set up a snow-fence barrier blocking the area where CBS had planned to put its camera. Minutes after we finished, a CBS vehicle showed up. They looked it over and drove away.

The next morning, the morning of the marathon, I noticed a CBS van next to the cannon at the starting line on the Verrazano Bridge. The van was empty, but it was rigged with some kind of transmitter gear on top. I smelled a rat. What if the personnel manning that vehicle made themselves scarce until right before the start and then climbed in and went on the air live? The van was in a perfect position to do that.

Over the sound system covering the starting area and the staging area at Fort Wadsworth, I paged CBS to come and move their van. Nobody came. I paged again. Still nobody. That year I had thirty guys with me, big, bouncer types, to help hold the crowds back at the start. I called them together and said, "We may have to move this van."

Then over the P.A. I announced: "If this truck is not moved within three minutes, it's going to be towed away by human bodies! And I cannot guarantee that it will be upright when we're finished!"

Suddenly two CBS people came scurrying up, jumped into the van, and zoomed away.

We had a magnificent race, the most dramatic competition we had ever had. Severe headwinds slowed the early pace, so we would have no world record this time. But Salazar and Rodolfo Gomez had a sensational duel from twenty miles on. From the Bronx, back into Manhattan, down Fifth Avenue, and into Central Park the two challenged each other, sometimes shoulder to shoulder, sometimes with one or the other surging into a short lead. Down the East Drive of Central Park, Salazar, mindful of Gomez' faster finishing kick, tried surge after surge—little bursts of speed—to try to soften up Gomez and strip him of his strength for a final kick. Each time Salazar surged, Gomez fought his way back to hang at his shoulder.

The two went across Central Park South and turned back into the park at Columbus Circle. Just inside the park there is a small section of turf the runners have to go over. The leading ABC camera vehicle went over the turf and threw up a cloud of dust. Within that cloud Salazar made his final surge.

That time, Gomez couldn't come back. Salazar beat him by four seconds.

On the women's side it was Grete Waitz again. Allison Roe was on the scene, but sidelined by injuries. Grete herself had suffered a stress fracture of her foot in July and had managed to put in only six weeks of good training before the race. She ran somewhat conservatively and won her fourth New York in a time of 2:27:14, almost a minute and a half ahead of Julie Brown.

The quality of our race and organization and media coverage all had a special significance that year, because we had bid to host several international competitions in 1983 and 1984. We bid to IAAF and TAC for the first Women's World Championship 10-K, which would be held in this country in the fall of 1983. We had already been awarded for the World Cross Country Championships—never before held in this country—scheduled for March 1984. And we bid to TAC for the men's and women's Olympic trials marathons for May 1984, from which the top three men and women would be selected for the Los Angeles Summer Olympics (where a women's marathon would be included for the first time).

The World Cross Country Championships has long been one of the most popular events in Europe, second only to the Olympics, drawing crowds of up to forty thousand. International cross-country, typically held at hippodromes (horse tracks) where runners have to pass over such barriers as tree trunks and steeplechase hurdles, includes a 5-K (3.1 miles) race for women and a 12-K (7.4 miles) race for men. I first saw the championships in 1979 in Limerick, Ireland, where I was recruiting for the marathon. Limerick is a city of 50,000, and they had a paying crowd of 25,000 for the championships. I loved the international pageantry, like a mini-Olympics. I thought, this event must come to the United States. With Gloria Averbuch, head of our media and promotion department, I went to the 1980 championships in Paris. Gloria put together our proposal, and at the 1981 championships in Madrid she presented the proposal to the IAAF, which approved it.

For the 1984 Olympic marathon trials our bid proposed a special course that started and ended in Central Park and wound around within Manhattan, designed so spectators in Central Park could see the runners pass four times.

We figured our demonstration of efficient success in recent years made us a natural host for these international events. But in the next few months politics and intrigues, too, would play a major role.

10

Politics hit the fan at the very opening of 1983. We thought, or hoped at least, that with the advent of the trust-fund system the hypocrisy issue would be laid to rest. Race organizers like us could award prize money openly and it would go into a trust fund—in this country administered by The Athletics Congress (TAC) and called TACTRUST. But in January, Alberto Salazar, the world's top marathoner, leveled a hot blast at TAC with an accusation that suggested the hypocrisy issue was alive and well.

Salazar accused TAC itself of offering him $60,000 in an attempt to lure him into a proposed spring Los Angeles marathon—an event from which TAC stood to gain $100,000 in consulting fees. TAC denied offering Salazar the money. Any offer to Salazar, TAC said, would have come, in proper fashion, from the race organizers.

In any case, Salazar was not going to run that marathon. Instead, International Management Group (IMG), the agency representing both Salazar and second-ranked Australian Rob de Castella, was trying to arrange a spring big-money "match race" between Salazar and de Castella in Australia or New Zealand. But the International Amateur Athletic Federation (IAAF), under whose rules national federations like TAC operate (and with whom TAC naturally had a very close and mutually supportive relationship), pressured both the Australian and the New Zealand federations not to sanction the special race.

But IMG wasn't to be denied. The agency arranged to match Salazar and de Castella against each other in the upcoming April Rotterdam Marathon, which was already sanctioned as a regularly scheduled race.

The proposed Los Angeles race, an abortive attempt by TAC to get into the race-promotion business, did not happen. But TAC was caught in a swirl of charges and countercharges involving IMG, the superagency that represented most of the world's top road runners and milers.

One issue underlying the Salazar-TAC feud was the fact that the first world championships of track and field (separate from the Olympics) were to be held in Helsinki, Finland, later in the year, and to go to the championships American runners had to run a qualifying marathon. The qualifying marathon for men was the Boston Marathon, also in April, a few days before Rotterdam. Salazar had asked TAC for a "bye" to go to the championships without running the qualifying marathon. TAC had refused to grant him an exemption.

Why did Salazar want a "bye"? One possible answer was supplied by TAC: Boston doesn't pay any money; Rotterdam was a money race; maybe Salazar was opting for the money. That angered Salazar enough for him to make his public charge about the $60,000 offer from TAC. After all, one major appeal of Rotterdam was that Salazar would have a chance to go head to head with de Castella.

But there was a more basic issue than just those marathons. Did TAC actually try to buy Salazar's appearance in a TAC-sanctioned event, and if so, was that to prevent IMG from taking him elsewhere? Did IAAF attempt to bar the "match race" to help TAC keep control over Salazar and to limit IMG's threatening growth of influence (international rules say agents should be discouraged from bargaining for their clients' participation in events)?

The fracas brought into the open a simmering power struggle for control over the entire world of road racing. With big money now being openly bargained for, the basic question was: If IAAF and national federations like TAC controlled the sanctions for the races, and IMG controlled the runners, who in fact controlled the sport?

We would get deeply embroiled in that struggle. It would be a year full of surprises.

Before the dust settled on the Salazar accusations, startling upsets shook up the world rankings. In Rotterdam on April 9 de Castella beat the previously undefeated Salazar convincingly in a time of 2:08:37—just twenty-four seconds off Salazar's 1981 world record—to become the top-ranked marathoner. Portugal's Carlo Lopes (who had dropped out of the 1982 New York after staying with Salazar for twenty miles) finished second, two seconds behind de Castella, to establish himself, in his first completed marathon, as one of the top runners in the world. Salazar finished fifth in 2:10:08, his slowest time ever.

On April 17 Grete Waitz tied Allison Roe's world record with a 2:25:29 in the London Marathon. On the very next day Joan Benoit, coach of women's long-distance running at Boston University, who had set the American record in 1982, smashed the world record with an astounding 2:22:43 in the Boston Marathon.

Another surprise of a different nature: We were denied the 1984 Olympic trials.

The trials are not an Olympic event per se, but are a regular TAC-sanctioned event run just like any other marathon, with the exception that there are qualifying times to get in, and TAC decides on the host city. I was on TAC's Site Selection Committee. Buffalo, New York, got the men's race. That wasn't greatly disturbing because they had done a good job with the 1980 trials.

Olympia, Washington, got the women's trials, and that was tougher to swallow.

When several cities made their bid presentations at the TAC convention the previous December in Philadelphia, the Olympia delegation had brought along a senator and spent a small fortune wining and dining and lobbying everybody; they said they had a

$1.2-million budget and a bunch of sponsors to cover it. We, on the other hand, were so confident that we would get either or both of the trials that we made a simple presentation and didn't bother lobbying at all. After all, we had the staff, the experience, the credentials. We were overconfident. I could sense an anti–New York backlash. The very image we tried to project—that we could showcase the events better than anybody else—worked against us; some people thought we were too hype-oriented.

For example, one person welcomed the selection of Buffalo over New York by writing: ". . . Thus the marathon trials will be conducted for the athletes, as they should, and not swamped in Big Apple hype and confusion." (However, the director of the Buffalo trials called that comment "inappropriate" and praised our capabilities in New York.)

It turned out that Olympia was swamped in hype and confusion. Avon, whose international women's running program had been instrumental in getting a women's marathon into the Olympics, wanted to sponsor the Olympia trials. Olympia's organizers turned Avon down, saying they preferred to have many sponsors rather than just one. But by the middle of 1983—less than a year from the event—they didn't have the necessary sponsorship, and they actually called me for help. About two hundred women would run the Olympia trials. You could put on an event like that beautifully for less than $400,000. By now they had scaled down their budget to $600,000 and still didn't have enough sponsorship to cover it. I didn't like the smell of the whole business, so I stayed out of it.

Meanwhile, we in New York had been busy from the first minute of the year. Our race calendar starts at the stroke of midnight with our New Year's Eve Run in Central Park. Sponsored by *The Runner* magazine and Brooks shoes, it's a 5-mile "fun run," complete with costumes, fireworks, and champagne, and draws three thousand runners. Nineteen eighty-three opened with a disaster. Though the park was closed to both automobiles and the famous horse-drawn hansom cabs, there was one horse-cab in the park near the starting line. When the fireworks went off at the start of the race, the horse bolted and charged into the mass of runners, sending thirteen to the hospital (one of those less seriously injured was Wendy Sly, Britain's top female miler).

Work on the marathon goes on year round, but by the time we accepted applications in the middle of the year, we had already put on dozens of events, including such major ones as:

• The L'eggs Mini Marathon 10-K, with 6,500 women; won by New Zealand's Anne Audain in an upset over Grete Waitz, who had won four straight times.

• The Trevira Twosome 10-mile couples' race, with 3,800 runners; won by the computer-matched team of England's Geoff Smith (a Providence College student soon to become a marathoner in our 1983 event) and Margaret Groos, of Oregon.

• The Perrier 10-K Run, with more than 5,000 runners; won by Geoff Smith (for the third straight time) and New York's Isabelle Carmichael.

• The TAC-USA Championship 100-Mile Run, held at Shea Stadium; won by Ray Scannell, of Massachusetts (New York's Stu Mittleman, holder of the American record of 12:56:34, was put out of the race with an injury), and New York's Donna Hudson, who set an American women's record of 15:31:57.

• The Empire State Building Run-Up; won by Al Waquie, a Pueblo Indian from New Mexico, in a time of 11 minutes 36 seconds.

• The annual series of three Manufacturers Hanover Corporate Challenge 3.5-mile races, each of which has a field of about 10,000 runners in corporate teams—an event that has spread to include other series we helped organize in several major cities.

• The Pepsi Challenge Championship 10-K, with 3,600 runners pouring across the George Washington Bridge from New Jersey to the Bronx; won by two New Zealanders, Rod Dixon (his second straight) and Anne Audain.

• Our first annual New York 6-Day Run. To resurrect a century-old event in which runners run, walk, eat, rest whenever they want, we erected a tent city in Downing Stadium on Randall's Island in the East River and provided round-the-clock kitchen, medical, and handling services for twenty-four elite ultramarathoners from six countries. It was won by Siegfried Bauer, of New Zealand, with 511 miles, and American records were set by Stu Mittleman (488 miles) and Lorna Richey, of Ohio (401 miles).

To the public the start of our marathon year is at midnight on June 1. There are two steps for entry: requests for entry blanks, and return of the completed entry forms. Requests for entry blanks must not be postmarked prior to June 1, so it has become a tradition for hopeful entrants to gather on the steps of the main post office at Eighth Avenue and 32nd Street long before midnight to get their requests for blanks in as early as possible. At midnight the post office opens up for us, and the hopefuls rush into the lobby to deposit their envelopes. In 1979, the first year we did this, a few hundred local runners gathered on the steps. By 1983 it had become thousands, and they came from everywhere.

The first person in line, a New York City fire marshal, arrived on the scene at 6 A.M. on May 31 and set up his folding chair for the long wait to midnight. By noon there were a couple of thousand, with lawn chairs and umbrellas and picnic lunches, radios, books, chess sets. By midnight more than six thousand people ringed the block.

Some of these people carried several envelopes for friends. We tried to restrict it to no more than five envelopes per person. To inhibit abuses, in 1983 we instituted a "handling charge" of three dollars for each entry-blank application. A few people protested that it was unfair to charge three dollars, since most of those paying the charge wouldn't get into the race (we would get 50,000 to 60,000 completed applications for 17,000 places). But we still had the expense of processing all those applications, and we had to do something to cut down on frivolous submissions. The previous year one person had sent in three hundred requests for application forms. I knew of at least five operations in the business of selling "guaranteed" entries.

In the line at the post office there were hustlers. One man had set up a business of charging customers ten dollars for standing in line for them—he even advertised nationwide to attract busi-ness. I was wandering around near the end of the line in the afternoon when a teenage boy came up to me and said, "Mister, for five dollars I'll wait in the line with your envelope."

So desperate were people for entry blanks that a fraud hap-pened within the post office itself. It was discovered, appropri-ately enough, by Joe Kleinerman, our registrar, a retired thirty-five-year veteran of the P.O. About 6 P.M. Joe went in to empty our boxes of all mail, to clear the way for the midnight avalanche. He found two bundles of mail—106 pieces—that turned out to be applications for entry blanks already postmarked "June 1." Joe figured that someone got paid off to preprocess this mail. Joe had it all repostmarked with the actual date, May 31, which meant that all those applications were voided for having jumped the June 1 deadline.

We take the applications for entry blanks on a first-come, first-served basis (foreign entries are handled separately). But to prevent all the spots going to New Yorkers, we send out the entry blanks in a staggered system—Far West first, then Midwest, then local. When the entry blanks are filled out and returned, with the ten-dollar entry fee, we accept the first 8,000. All the rest go into the lottery drawing in August. (We also have a waiting-list procedure: Anyone who is accepted, but then notifies us before October 10 that he or she is withdrawing, is guaranteed entry into next year's race.)

By the end of June we had 50,000 applications for marathon entry blanks (thousands more poured in for weeks after that). We mailed out the first blanks on June 26. On June 29 we started receiving completed entries—3,000 the first day. By July 2 we had the first 8,000. From then on, everybody went into the lottery.

This year we were determined to cut our marathon losses. Every year the marathon had lost money. We had deficits of $79,000 in 1981 and $65,000 in 1982. A budget of $1.3 million for 1983 might seem like a lot. But half that goes right off the top for things we provide free for all the runners—the premarathon pasta party and postmarathon disco party, shorts and T-shirts

and other items in their registration packets, calligraphed certifi-
cates and medals to finishers—all amounting to more than $40
per runner. We give away about $15,000 worth of T-shirts and
souvenirs to assorted bigwigs—city officials, sponsors, foreign
dignitaries, press. We pay all expenses for about 130 elite invited
runners and prize money for the top 20 male finishers and top 15
females. What might seem like inconsequential items cost
plenty. The bleachers are not free (tents, tables, bleachers,
$65,000); the portable toilets are not free (toilets and trailers,
$19,500); the silver Mylar thermal blankets are not free
($40,000); and so on.

And one of the major things that set us apart from other
marathons—city support—though inordinately generous in ways
beyond what money can measure, is not totally free. Our marathon is a fully cooperative venture. The city shares in our
television revenues. We sponsor an Emergency Medical Services
ambulance. We contribute to such park improvements as fencing, signs, water fountains. From our 1983 marathon budget we
donated a substantial amount of money to the Department of
Parks and Recreation.

Publicity is essential to call attention to the NYRRC so we can
spread the gospel and benefit of running to the general public.

As part of our mandate from the city to be the organization
providing running events as a social service, we have losses
programmed into our overall budget throughout the year. To
avoid overcommercialism, we do not have sponsors for most of
our races. Profit from some of our sponsored races allows us to
put on the unsponsored races and other events—such as clinics,
exhibits, the Urban Running Program, the prison programs.
Other losses are not by design, but are acceptable as invest-
ments. We lost more than $50,000 on the 6-Day Run because I
couldn't sell it for sponsorship by advertisers. But we got a ton of
publicity (including live nightly coverage from ABC, on Ted
Koppel's popular *Nightline* show), so I could assume that it
would attract sponsors for subsequent years. We would lose a
bundle on the 1984 World Cross Country Championships, but

the prestige of hosting that event for the first time in the United States overweighed bottom-line considerations.

The marathon was developed in the same vein. The idea was to make it happen, make it grow, make it excellent—without focusing on the bottom line. Quality was, and is, our highest priority, and that includes quality of sponsorship. In the long run it is a better investment to have appropriate sponsorship than just any sponsorship. We once turned down one of the biggest fast-food chains for race sponsorship because I felt it was the wrong image for us. We turned down one of the most prominent designer-clothes manufacturers because they were too blatantly money-oriented, high-pressure, and flamboyant. They had with great fanfare sponsored some earlier open-prize-money races in various places which got many athletes in trouble for defying amateur rules. They were so determined to play a role here that whether they became a sponsor or not, they wanted to give a six-figure prize to our marathon winner (we nixxed that plan, too).

We have a tradition of reciprocal loyalty with our major sponsors—Manufacturers Hanover, Perrier, the Rudin family, Inner City Broadcasting (of which former Manhattan Borough President Percy Sutton, our original booster, is chairman), *The Runner* magazine. The loyalty is not based solely on how much money they pay, but on their steadfast support and willingness to carry a fair share of the load according to ability to pay.

But the reality is that our costs rise annually, and annually we have to try to wheedle more money. One of those major sponsors whose name had a particularly privileged place on the finish-line banner had been paying $75,000 for the last two years and intended to stay with that amount in 1983. I insisted that in fairness they should increase their contribution by $16,000. They resisted. They suggested a compromise: They would give us $8,000 more, and we could move their name to a less-favored position on the banner. There was no question that they could afford the $16,000 (they still would not be our biggest sponsor). And I couldn't believe that for a few thousand dollars they would give up a banner position that was worth a fortune in publicity (the more central the banner position, the more often it appears in photos and on TV). In truth, I could sell their choice position immediately to another sponsor for five times what they were paying. But I preferred to maintain our relationship. Eventually, they agreed to the higher increase.

A crucial breakthrough in 1983 was the arrival of MDS Qantel, Inc., the computer company. We worked out a five-year deal with them for more than $300,000 in equipment and consulting services. With their system we would have instantly available on the computer terminals details not only on every club member but on every runner who entered our races, including racing history, best times, hometown, age, occupation. In addition to that, the system would be used year-round at the club for financial management, word processing, invoicing. We would be totally independent from any outside computer services. Qantel, already the "Official Computer of the National Basketball Association," now became the "Official Computer of the New York City Marathon." Thus, our 1983 marathon would be the most highly computerized and best documented road race in history.

Seiko, the Japanese watch company, continued for the second year as official timer; Kappa Sports remained for the third year as supplier of outfits for our race officials. Hertz Corporation was also back as sponsor for the third year.

The New York–New Jersey Buick Dealers Association was interested in supplying the lead cars, and when I first met with them I asked for $75,000. They thought that was outrageous. To demonstrate my confidence in the value of the lead cars, I made a proposition. I said to Buick: "You give me nothing, and I'll give *you* ten thousand dollars. You provide the lead vehicles for the marathon and then hire an independent analyst to decide what it was worth. I'll take ten percent of that figure. Because I think an independent analyst would say the publicity and exposure are worth one million." (In fact, for the following year's marathon we would get offers as high as $200,000 from car companies that wanted their vehicles to lead the marathon.) Eventually we settled on $50,000, plus the use of a car for a year. Buick would supply as lead cars two customized white Riviera convertibles.

Besides major sponsors, we have a category of "supporters," who provide lesser amounts of money or services in exchange for being included in our publicity. In July I was visited by a representative of Moosehead Beer, of Canada, which wanted to expand its New York market. They thought that participation in our marathon was a good way to do it. Mindful of the Parks Department's earlier antipathy to beer sponsorship, I wasn't sure we could get away with accepting Moosehead, but I discussed it anyway, to feel out the situation. To be a sponsor, I said, might cost $150,000. He said they didn't have that kind of money. I said that they might consider being a "supporter" for about $20,000; maybe they could supply the beer at the pasta party or disco party, both of which get a lot of press coverage. That seemed possible. He said he would talk it over with company officials.

I thought it would be interesting to test the waters with a low-key beer company. If they came back with an offer, I would leave it up to the Good Taste Committee (headed by Jack Rudin, and including the parks commissioner and other sponsors) to decide.

We got them for the pasta party, which was safe because the party would be held in a private office building.

Strengthening our sponsorship and list of supporters was essential. We needed money. Although our growth was impressive to outsiders, the fact remained that we didn't have enough money inside. Our staff was still woefully underpaid. And in the summer of 1983 that was one of the reasons we almost lost Allan Steinfeld.

Kathy Switzer asked Allan to come to work for her as manager of Avon's international women's running program. It was a very prestigious job, for considerably more money, vacation time, corporate perks—all the things we had been unable to provide. I wasn't going to stand in his way if he wanted to leave. On the other hand, as even Kathy acknowledged, there were enormous future possibilities for Allan within our own organization if we could turn the corner financially. Those possibilities were not just more income; they included opportunities for national and international operations suitable to a man of Allan's talents.

We were all sacrificing financially for the enjoyments and challenges of our operation. A couple of years before, I had been offered a six-figure job with a clothing company, but I turned it down because all it meant, after all, was more money for me. More money would have been nice, but more important was the fact that there were still too many dramatic things left to accomplish with what we were doing and planning.

Allan was cut from the same cloth. Still, he agonized over the decision. One of the immediate things troubling him was that he was getting ever more bogged down with day-to-day responsibilities that sapped his time and energy. To ease that load, we made Bill Noel, a former corporate executive who had been with us for several years, third in command, utilizing his executive skills by giving him responsibility for personnel matters, building operation, and direction of more events. (Noel was also a track and field official at the Olympics.) Allan would continue to have overall direction under me, but could concentrate on more major projects, such as directing the World Cross Country Championships and serving as technical consultant to races around the world.

To the relief of all of us, Allan chose to stay. He knew as well as I that not very far down the road we could be looking at significantly increased revenues from television and Madison Avenue which would allow us to operate more comfortably.

Also in the summer I got caught up in heavy politicking between International Management Group and TAC. A few months before, IMG and TAC had barely been on speaking terms, largely because of the Salazar–Los Angeles Marathon squabble. We were sort of in the middle because we had to deal with both organizations. All of a sudden I got wind that IMG and TAC were buddying up, and it was going to be at our expense.

After we had invested a great deal in setting up a 5th Avenue Mile–type circuit in cities around the world, IMG seemed suddenly to be trying to take the world circuit away from us and go it alone with their own milers, their own TV and sponsor deals—and with the endorsement and financial partnership of TAC. With the chance that these mile runs were finally going to be profitable, it looked as if they were trying to cut us out.

It spread to marathons. At about this same time IMG started leaning on me about Salazar. Both Chicago and Las Vegas wanted Salazar for their prize-money marathons, which were going to be TAC-sanctioned, I was told, and it was time for me to play ball with a money offer that Salazar and TAC would accept.

I protested to TAC. First of all, I told TAC that the world mile circuit was ours; we had thought it up, organized it, developed it. We would fight any attempt to preempt it, even if we ended up in court about it. Furthermore, I resented IMG using other marathons—especially the Las Vegas Marathon—to apply leverage on me, with the implication that TAC was a party to it.

Some time earlier a Hollywood filmmaker named Gary Stromberg had approached me for advice about his notion to promote a "Million Dollar Marathon" in Las Vegas. There would be $1 million, either for a world record or in a lottery among entrants. I had told him that I doubted that TAC would approve such a gross prize—that TAC *shouldn't* approve it—and hence he wouldn't get big runners or TV. Beyond that, I offered no advice. I didn't want to get involved.

So now I told TAC that as far as marathons were concerned, Chicago could do whatever it wanted, but the Las Vegas proposition was bad for the sport and shouldn't receive TAC support. In any case, whatever TAC supported shouldn't be used as leverage against us. If TAC tied in too closely with the biggest agency representing runners, and our survival was threatened, we would take whatever steps necessary to protect ourselves and our program.

My attitude upset TAC. But I wasn't threatening them. I just wanted them to know they couldn't mess around with us. We were one of the most important organizations in the country in our support and cooperation with TAC. So I was cashing in some of my chips, and I felt it was in the best interests of the sport.

When IMG heard about my words with TAC, they accused me

of politicking behind *their* backs. I said I was indeed politicking, and would continue to politick, because while I liked to see an accommodation between IMG and TAC instead of warfare, it was in nobody's interests to have a monopoly. And IMG was coming dangerously close to having that. The problem, I told them, was that IMG was the only game in town. They owned the top milers, and we needed them for the 5th Avenue Mile; they owned the top marathoners, and we needed them for our marathon; they owned the top 10-K women, and we needed them for the Mini Marathon. With no competition they were in a position to dictate which events would have their clients, and hence which events would be successful. If TAC acquiesced in that, the whole grassroots foundation for the sport of road running could dry up.

And so we were holding our ground. We would deal, but we would not take dictation. That seemed to temper any grand-scale maneuvering for the time being, as far as we were concerned, anyway.

Shortly after that, Salazar's agent approached me to bargain specifically for Salazar. He said that Salazar had been offered $80,000 to run in yet another Los Angeles marathon, this one scheduled for three weeks before New York, and he wanted me to meet the price. (Funny thing about marathons touted for L.A. by somebody or other: There's always big money involved, and the marathons seldom happen. In the last couple of years five or six big marathons hyped for L.A. haven't come off.)

I didn't know whether this latest one was likely or not, but I reminded the agent that Salazar wasn't Number One anymore— Rob de Castella was—so his negotiating strength wasn't what it had been, and further that Salazar should weigh carefully the relative overall commercial value of running in L.A. as opposed to New York. I said our limit for Salazar would be $20,000, a firm maximum.

I got a call from Bob Bright, director of the Chicago Marathon. He wanted to make a deal. If I would lay off Carlos Lopes (who finished second to de Castella in Rotterdam, with the fifth fastest time ever), he would not fight me for Salazar. At that point it looked like Lopes was a better runner than Salazar. De Castella was probably not going to run a marathon in the United States in the fall (likely he would choose Fukuoka instead). That left Lopes as perhaps the best of the available lot.

I knew I wasn't going to make the deal with Bright, but instead of rejecting it outright, I stalled. (My usual philosophy: Listen, stall, gain time to reassess.) Bright and I were both going to be in Helsinki in August for the world championships. I told him we could discuss it there.

Then I got a call from a representative of Lopes, in Portugal. He told me Chicago had offered Lopes $5,000 appearance money, to go with $20,000 prize money to the winner, and a bonus of about $15,000 for a world record. But he said that Lopes would prefer to run New York. He wanted to know what our scale was. I told him we would give $25,000 for a win and a $25,000 bonus for a world record, but I didn't want to commit myself on appearance money. Actually, I wasn't offering anybody appearance money except Salazar, whom I had promised $20,000. But I wanted to leave it open on Lopes. I told the guy that Lopes could rest assured we'd take good care of him and his wife if he ran New York.

At the end of July we got our first direct indication that CBS was interested in capturing the marathon from ABC. Robert Ingraham, vice-president of Capital Sports, Inc., which produces events for television, told me that CBS, to whom his company had marketed the Tour de France bicycle race, "wants the New York City Marathon real bad" and would consider a package deal to cover other events such as the 5th Avenue Mile and our planned first New York Triathalon. Because of the confidentiality clause in our contract, we couldn't reveal how much ABC was paying or even how long the contract ran. "Even if CBS went over one million," I said, "I don't think ABC would let the marathon go." Regardless, Ingraham said, CBS's interest would surely force the price up, and we would benefit—to which I was pleased to agree.

When they started wining and dining us with obvious intentions and expectations for 1984, we finally had to tell them that the marathon was not available that year. That was a shock. Fortunately, though, they expressed their interest in the years beyond, and still wanted to pursue the 1984 triathalon, which we were trying to put together to present to the city for approval.

On August 2, 1983, we held our symbolic marathon-entry lottery drawing on the steps of City Hall. There was a lot of press as usual, and a combo wearing New York City Marathon caps played tunes around the "I Love New York" theme. Mayor Koch and new Parks Commissioner Henry Stern spoke about their expectations for another great marathon, and then Bill Rodgers—saying that the New York City Marathon was "the most important big-city marathon in the world"—drew the first ten lottery selections from a big drum.

Immediately after the festivities, though, my high spirits were suddenly dampened. An intermediary delivered to me a private and disturbing directive from Mayor Koch: Koch was forbidding us once again to offer open prize money.

Our bad luck stemmed from events of a couple of weeks before. The city had permitted singer Diana Ross to give a free concert in Central Park. A crowd of 350,000 had attended the concert, and then gangs of young toughs leaving the concert marauded through the streets, mugging and vandalizing. The cost to the city for police and cleanup was more than $500,000. What's more, the concert had been taped for presentation on a cable network—indicating a possible good profit for Ross and the organizers. And now the mayor was taking heat for allowing such commercialization of an event that turned sour at high cost to the city.

So to avoid further protests about commercialism of city-supported events, the mayor was banning the marathon from giving open prize money. Not only that, the intermediary told me, but I was not to say the mayor banned it. Nor would there be any discussion; for the mayor it was a closed issue.

That put me in a very difficult position because this year we would have to file a prize-money plan with TAC in order to get a sanction for the marathon—just as other marathons were doing. After having told people that we would be giving prize money, I had to retract that and again publicly deny it. As much as I had worked to end it, hypocrisy was back. Plus I had to come up with some plausible new explanation for why all of a sudden we weren't giving prize money.

The second week of August I went to Helsinki for the world track and field championships. Rob de Castella won the men's marathon and Grete Waitz the women's. But the main event for me was politics.

Bob Bright was there, passing out cards publicizing the prize-money structure of his Chicago Marathon, which was to be in October, a week before ours—a total of $135,000, including $20,000 each for the men's and women's winners. Not only was he trying to attract top athletes to his race, but with the publicity he was also issuing an implicit challenge to us to similarly publicize our prize money. I couldn't, because Mayor Koch had banned me from doing it, and I couldn't say he banned me from it. In a real bind, I came up with the idea to lay it off on the possible danger to the Olympics. Ever since the IAAF's adoption of the trust-fund system, no Russians or East Germans had been willing to compete in prize-money races.

There was a meeting of the board of directors of AIMS, the forty-one-member Association of International Marathons (which we founded four years earlier, and of which I was vice-president and Allan was chairman of the Standards Committee), to discuss, among other things, the possibility for urging that a cap be put on amounts of prize money that could be paid—to keep the money business from going totally out of control. I used the opportunity to announce that while we had made no firm decision, many track and field officials had pleaded with me not to give prize money in New York this year because the Russians and East Germans might use the money as an excuse to boycott the Olympic marathon in 1984 if it included runners who had won money in New York. I said that these officials felt it was all right for Chicago to do it, but not New York, because New York had such high visibility around the world.

Having temporarily slipped that problem, I was made furious over another: IAAF President Primo Nebiolo made an out-of-the-blue announcement that the first Women's World Championship 10-K, sanctioned by IAAF and TAC, and sponsored by Avon, would be held in San Diego. I had been so sure we were going to get it in New York that we had printed it in our schedule. Kathy Switzer of Avon, who was also in Helsinki, hadn't even been informed of the decision—and Avon hadn't yet officially committed itself to sponsorship. I couldn't believe such a decision could be so arbitrarily made and inappropriately announced.

I got involved in yet another flap, this one over the 5th Avenue Mile. British runner Steve Cram won the 1,500 meters in Helsinki, and we immediately invited him to run the 5th Avenue Mile on September 3. Then an Italian IAAF official complained to Ollan Cassell, executive director of TAC, that the 5th Avenue Mile was siphoning off too many of the world's top milers during the time of the European track-mile circuit—specifically two Italian mile races. Cassell and I hadn't been seeing eye to eye on a few things lately, one of them being our independence in the conducting of the 5th Avenue Mile. I didn't want to alienate him or the IAAF further, so I worked out a compromise with the Italian official. For the 5th Avenue Mile we could have Eamonn Coghlan (indoor-mile-record holder and winner of the 5,000 meters in Helsinki), American Steve Scott (second to Cram in the Helsinki 1,500 meters), Sydney Maree (our 1981 winner), and American Tom Byers (our 1982 winner); we would let him have Steve Cram and a couple of top Spanish milers he wanted.

The deal wouldn't have aggravated anybody if I hadn't taken it a step further. I let *The New York Times* know about it, and they printed it.

When we got back to New York, Allan and I had a fairly heated meeting with TAC lawyer Alvin Chriss, focusing on the intrigues of Helsinki. Chriss administers the TACTRUST and is generally the spokesman for Ollan Cassell. Chriss is also an old friend and a member of our club. He has a brusque and straightforward manner and is often cast in the delicate role of mediating between us and Cassell. One of the smartest things Cassell did as TAC executive director may have been to hire Chriss to run interference and see to hammering out difficult details of arrangements with race directors.

But that didn't mean we didn't have some pretty rough haggling at times with Chriss. At issue now were the politics in Helsinki and our relationship with TAC and Cassell. Chriss hadn't liked seeing the item in the *Times* about the 5th Avenue Mile, which revealed a bit of independent wheeling and dealing for runners in the international arena. He warned us about not being deferential enough to Cassell and reminded us that Cassell was the boss of running in this country, not me, and that I needed him. "Ollan feels that you don't keep him informed of anything ahead of time," Chriss said.

I wasn't in the mood for stroking. "Ollan has been trying to get money for TAC by buddying up with IMG on the world mile circuit," I said, "but he won't lift a finger to help us with the 5th Avenue Mile. We work hard to get sponsors and runners, but maybe IMG is the boss because they control all the runners. And you let them get away with it."

Chriss allowed that IMG could be a problem and that the relationship among TAC and IMG and us was touchy and intricate. But he stressed that Ollan had the real power, whether I liked it or not; it was TAC, after all, that would grant sanctions for the 5th Avenue Mile and the marathon and everything else.

I fired back that the 5th Avenue Mile was ours and that we would continue to make it a success with or without TAC.

Then I vented my anger over the sudden choice of San Diego over New York for the TAC-sanctioned women's 10-K World Championship, scheduled for late fall. "Kathy Switzer didn't even know about it," I said, "and Ollan's only response to that was that the sponsor doesn't determine where TAC events are held, TAC does. What kind of an attitude is that? Kathy wants it in New York." (Chriss and I both knew that some of her bosses were leaning toward Dallas, in order to parade the event under the noses of Mary Kay Cosmetics, Avon's competition, which is headquartered there.) "San Diego is a terrible choice."

Chriss defended San Diego because of its weather and the fact that the mayor "will lay out the red carpet for us." He said the whole city would be dominated, *"owned"* by the event. After all, he said, San Diego wasn't exactly nowhere—it was the eighth largest city in the country.

"So who wants number eight when you can have number one?" I said. "Here I could guarantee you big television coverage, big crowds, everything. You hold that event in San Diego, I can tell you the national coverage will be a total of a two-inch story by AP."

Chriss acknowledged that the Helsinki announcement might have been premature. But it remained clear that San Diego had the big edge, not the least of reasons for which was the appearance (in TAC's eyes) that New York got too much attention and that TAC needed to demonstrate that it could put on a major event someplace else.

Next came the matter of marathon prize money, and here Chriss wanted to be an ally. TAC would be giving us a sanction this year. We had already been notified officially by letter from Chriss that, pursuant to international rules pertaining to Olympic eligibility, Ollan Cassell "has strongly recommended to you that in 1983, the New York City Marathon adopt an open 'prize' money structure and apply for a TACTRUST sanction permitting such funds to be paid to athletes without impairment of international eligibility."

Since we had not done that before, Chriss asked me how we were going to handle it. I told him about the mayor vetoing it and prohibiting me from saying he did so.

"You think I should talk to him?" Chriss asked.

"No," I said. "I wasn't supposed to tell you. I don't know how to get around it."

Chriss suggested that maybe we could just make a donation to TAC in the amount of the prize money, and TAC would write checks for the athletes.

"We're talking about a quarter of a million dollars," I said. "Somebody shows the press a check for prize money from TAC, they're going to ask where the money came from. We'd never get away with it."

He cautioned me that Bob Bright, of Chicago, was likely to be a real problem for New York. "He will battle you on this, Fred, he will try to blow it open. With his open prize money and a TAC sanction, he will do everything he can to really challenge you, try to force your hand on this." So, he said, if I told the press with my "usual wink" that I wasn't giving prize money, the press, encouraged by Bright's example, would ask Chriss why New York wasn't giving prize money. And then Chriss would have to admit that TAC had in fact given New York permission to pay prize money based on a prize-money structure we would have submitted. We were in a real jam.

"There's no other way," Chriss said. "Koch has to be straightened out."

"Koch won't even talk about it," I said. "He doesn't want to hear about it. He refuses to have it commercialized openly because of the Diana Ross thing. And there's nothing I can do about that."

Chriss understood and was sympathetic. After thinking a minute he said: "Okay. If I'm asked, the best thing I can do is hedge, say 'No comment.' I'm willing to do that for you. But then you have to keep quiet, too, Fred. You can't say anything that puts us in a bad light. You cannot make TAC the whipping boy on this. If you do, the deal's off."

11

Every year, a few weeks before the marathon, we hold our Baked Apple Run, a jaunt over the entire course, with a police escort and several rest stops, for staffers and a few invited guests. For those of us who have to work during our marathon and so can't run in it, it is our only chance to experience the course from the runners' viewpoint.

This is also the day of our final official course measurement. All of our courses are measured for official certification, using bicycles calibrated precisely before and after each race. No course is measured with greater care than the marathon course. Our experts, such as Bill Noel, director of operations for the club, and course coordinator for the marathon, are called upon internationally to measure courses.

In the wee hours of the morning of this year's Baked Apple, Noel, accompanied by our librarian, Mimi Fahnestock, and a few others set out to measure the course. Their bikes were equipped with special wheel-revolution counters called Jones Devices (named after the man who invented the device ten years ago and which we now manufacture and sell around the world). Beginning at the finish line in Central Park, they took more than four hours to trace the route, noting each exact mile mark, to the start on the Staten Island end of the Verrazano Bridge. When they finally brought their bikes to a halt at the precise spot they would designate as the starting line, the 26-mile 385-yard course was accurate to within a few yards.

Then a few dozen of us, accompanied by a police escort and trailed by a medical crew carrying refreshments and buses to pick up stragglers, set out to run the Baked Apple along the freshly remeasured course. I ran most of it, but not all, at a slow pace.

Through all the complications and big events of 1983, I had been keeping up my own marathon schedule—which as usual would include one final one to tire out my legs before our own marathon. It had been a lousy year. In January I ran my worst ever on American soil, a 4:40 in the Orange Bowl Marathon in Miami. In February I ran another slow one in New Orleans. Then I had a series of debacles.

For the Shanghai Marathon in March I had trained hard, was in great shape, ready to run my best in years. I even thought my best ever—a 3:29 in Syracuse, New York, in 1970—was within reach. It was a small field of about five hundred runners. The Chinese treated me as an honored guest and insisted over my objections that I line up with the fastest runners in the very front row, where they had painted on the road a number "6" matching my running number.

At the same time the gun went off, I was distracted trying to set my stopwatch. I got knocked down by runners behind me and landed hard on my shoulder. Everybody ran over me, trampled me—there was no way to avoid me in the beginning surge. I was hurt, but I wasn't about to drop out right at the start. So I walked a little, then began running. The whole pack of them were far ahead. Crowds along the way were laughing at me—this westerner running dead-last way behind the field. After ten kilometers I was in such agony from my shoulder that I pulled off to the side. The course here was in farmland, and I saw this old guy carrying two pails of water on a bamboo pole over his shoulder. I waved him over and tried to indicate how my shoulder hurt and that I wanted him to dump a refreshing pail of water over me. But he got behind me, grabbed my shoulders, and pushed his knee into my back. There was a brief moment of tremendous, sharp pain, then magically my shoulder was better.

I ran on okay until about five kilometers from the finish, and the agony returned. I just about collapsed, but managed to finish in 4:28—last. They took me to the hospital, X-rayed me, spread something that looked like plum jelly around my shoulder and arm, and gave me mysterious but extremely potent pills of which I was to take four (three brown and one yellow) three times a day. The pain didn't return until I ran out of pills a few days later. Back in New York, the doctor said I had probably suffered a slight shoulder dislocation, and he put my arm in a sling. (Examining the last of my Chinese pills, he said they were not something he could prescribe, but that I could sell them for a lot on the street.)

For the Rome Marathon, in April, I was again feeling good. New Zealand's Allison Roe, then the women's world-record holder, was their biggest "name" entrant, so they built the publicity around her. She and I had dinner the night before, fettucini Alfredo and banana splits, at a new hotel. About 2 A.M. she called me in my room to ask how I felt—she was sick as a dog. I felt fine, except that I wasn't able to sleep. The rest of the night Allison got all kinds of medical attention. It would be a disaster for the race organizers if she couldn't run.

She couldn't. By race time, in the morning, she was still woefully sick. I still felt okay. Halfway into the race it hit me. I got so nauseous that I had to stop. I lay down on a grassy area beside the road and fell asleep. I slept for about an hour. When I woke up, I felt as good as new. There were still a few of the slowest runners straggling by. I rejoined the race and ran hard to the finish. I felt terrific, but my time, including the nap, was 4:57— my all-time worst, but at least I wasn't dead last.

By the day of the Paris Marathon, in May, my only problem was that an old knee injury had flared up. Five hours before the start, scheduled for early evening, I decided a massage would be good to loosen up my knee. Instead, I found a Jacuzzi in the hotel. After ten minutes in this wonderful Jacuzzi with very powerful jets, my knee felt better. So I stayed in it an hour. I couldn't have been more relaxed. When I came out, I noticed a sign I hadn't seen before. It said there was a five-minute limit in the Jacuzzi because it was so powerful.

Right after the start of the marathon, I was running on empty. I had been totally drained of energy. I managed to continue half the distance before I staggered off and caught the Métro back to the hotel. It was the first time after twenty-six straight marathons that I failed to finish.

The year was going so badly that I decided to skip a couple of months. I had built up a cushion on my schedule by running twenty-six marathons in the last twenty-four months, so I could still keep my overall marathon-a-month pace.

The layoff didn't help much. In August I ran the Helsinki Marathon (a regular marathon held during the week of the track and field championships). Another poor job: 4:24.

I was so dissatisfied that I might not have run another marathon that year, except that there was one more I *had* to run. So as not to be any more frustrated than I am at not being able to run in our own marathon, I always run one just before ours, so that at least my legs will be tired. The one I picked in 1983 was Berlin, at the end of September.

Though I had never run the Berlin Marathon, I had a special feeling for it because it was one of those that I had helped develop.

In 1979 and 1980 people began drawing on our successful experience to develop their own marathons. San Francisco, for example, was running their marathon in Golden Gate Park, and the organizers wanted to bring it into the city. I was invited there to help them convince Mayor Dianne Feinstein that it could be done, and how it could be done. They did it, it was successful. (In fact, in 1983 their marathon suddenly doubled in size, to about 10,000, and Allan Steinfeld was summoned out there to help them redesign their finish-line system to accommodate that field.)

In 1979 British journalist Chris Brasher, the gold medalist in the 1956 Olympic steeplechase, came to New York to run our marathon. He was so impressed that he wrote an article in *The*

Observer, saying that London should be able to do what New York had done. In 1980 London did host the Avon Women's Marathon, which I was there to see. The police and other government officials thought the race was so complicated and difficult that the idea of holding an even bigger marathon on an annual basis was unworkable. I did my best to convince them otherwise. That October a delegation of British observers, including the London chief of police, came over to witness our race, and they became believers. The first London Marathon was held in 1981, with Chris Brasher as director and a field of seven thousand runners. I was flattered to be given the number "1," but I had to drop out at eighteen miles because of a knee problem.

That first year they had a terrible backup at the finish line. For the next year they asked Allan to come over and advise them on how to improve their system. Their subsequent marathon, the largest in the world (still the only one bigger than ours), with eighteen thousand starters, worked beautifully. Chris Brasher works closely with us now as president of the Association of International Marathons.

In Berlin organizers had been trying unsuccessfully to bring a woodland marathon into downtown West Berlin. At the Stockholm Marathon, in 1980, the Berlin Marathon director complained to me that he couldn't get the cooperation of the government. I suggested he cut through to the heart of the matter: Get the chief of police on his side; make a personal friend of him, invite him to dinner, familiarize himself with the special problems and orientation the police have. And then, I told the director, invite the chief of police to come with him to observe the New York City Marathon—we can set it up so that he can learn everything he needs to know.

The result was that the marathon was moved into downtown West Berlin. I would run Berlin as my twenty-eighth marathon in twenty-eight months, my fifty-fifth overall.

The race was efficiently organized for the field of six thousand runners, with lots of nice touches (I'm always on the lookout for things we might incorporate in New York): dozens of flags flying; several long rows of cots for pre-race and post-race massages;

roses to be given every female finisher—an idea that I instantly adopted for the upcoming New York.

It was a beautiful cool day, and once again I felt ready to try for a good time—to break four hours, at least. When the gun went off at 9 A.M. sharp, amid the friendly, festive atmosphere, I suddenly had a strange feeling. The start was on the actual lawn of the historic Reichstag building, rebuilt after the war. I thought: This country is responsible for the holocaust that screwed up my childhood and family life—I'm running on their turf—I'm going to show them.

It was a private thought, and I felt a little uncomfortable about it because it wasn't a fair reflection on my hosts, or the whole congenial atmosphere of the event, but still it spurred me. I ran hard. After twenty miles it was clear that I would finish in well under four hours. When at last I saw the finish banner and clock right in the middle of Berlin, I saw I had a chance to break 3:40. I began a long sprint, driving myself. I finished in 3:39:02, my best time in more than ten years. And then I threw up.

At the awards ceremony the chief of police was given a deserved medal for his efforts (the control of crowds and traffic was the best I had seen). And I was presented a wristwatch for my contributions to their marathon.

Satisfied in mind and body, I was ready to return home and dive into the final frantic preparations for our own marathon.

The 1983 New York City Marathon would be the biggest, the most complex, and the most dramatic that we had ever had. But in the last weeks before the event there is so much going on at once that it is difficult to sense whether everything is coming together right. Details come in a torrent, and we don't dare ignore any of them because we never know when little details will suddenly become big problems.

There were meetings upon meetings, with Parks and Police and other city departments, with ABC and sponsors; we were dealing with invited runners and with rejected runners appealing for places; we were holding press conferences and interviews; we were straightening out computers and technical foulups. Despite our experience and our pattern for procedures, every year it is like a brand-new game; things that go right one year go wrong the next, and vice versa. And there are always innovations as yet untested in the marathon. In the first weeks of October our aim is to get most things under control so that by the time we move into our marathon headquarters in the Sheraton Centre Hotel for Marathon Week, we can concentrate on registration of runners and the race itself.

Our park coordinator, Raleigh Mayer, a young woman in her first year with the club, was grappling with the logistics for Central Park: tents, tables, trucks, trailers, parking permits, where everything was supposed to be, and when it was supposed to be there. Beyond that, Alice Cashman, director of special events for the Parks Department, was worried about a shortage of barricades for crowd control (I had the idea of importing French-made metal barricades, common all over Europe, to supplement the city's wooden ones); about helicopters (last year two police helicopters had landed on the lawn near the finish line to conserve fuel—police assured her that wouldn't happen again); about a more efficient public-address system to control the crowd at the finish line and direct people to the Family Reunion Area, where runners can be met after they finish (Allan had already arranged for a new system); about tighter security for the reviewing stand so that important politicians would be let in and not everybody else (a member of the mayor's staff would see to that).

Even park aesthetics were involved—always a high priority. Cashman was annoyed that the blue line was still visible on the park road from the year before. "We don't want to be looking at a blue line in Central Park three hundred and sixty-five days a year," she said. This year I would try to use a thinner paint in the park so it would wear away quicker under traffic.

The police, too, were concerned about the barricade shortage. People steal them, chop them up for firewood, and there had been a strike at the Consolidated Edison utility company, which usually makes a lot of our barricades. There were two thousand barricades available, one thousand less than last year. At first the Parks Department didn't want to accept my offer to import metal barricades (city agencies tend to be conservative, wary of new ideas). But with police encouragement they went along. We spent $37,000 on the metal barricades.

The police have become very sophisticated about the marathon and have compiled a complete book of procedures they follow— exact descriptions of positions and routes of vehicles, precise timetables for arrival at intersections throughout the course, assignment of personnel, instructions for special escorts, and so forth.

The lead formation would be tightened up this year. Instead of the first "outrider" group of five motorcycles being three miles (fifteen minutes) ahead of the race, they would be two miles (ten minutes) ahead. Tow trucks would accompany that first group— they can remove a disabled or illegally parked car in minutes. Each intersection would be officially closed when that first outrider group arrived. The upper roadway of the Verrazano Bridge would be closed to traffic at 3 A.M. on race day, to allow our preparations for the start.

As usual, this year police representatives were coming from several places, including Amsterdam, San Francisco, and Los Angeles (where they needed to learn all they could before the Olympics), to observe our police procedures at the marathon.

We held our first press conference to announce the entry of two notables (mixing as we often do runners and other celebrities), New Zealand Olympian Rod Dixon and former world heavyweight boxing champion Floyd Patterson. Dixon, thirty-three, was the bronze medalist in the 1,500 meters at the 1972 Olympics and was once top ranked in the world at 5,000 meters. He had run only one marathon, but that was at world-class speed—a 2:11:21 in Auckland the previous year. His range of world-class speed from the mile to the marathon made him unique. In the previous year he had run nineteen races, at less than marathon distance, and won them all. Not only did he predict victory here, but he said, "I'm in the best shape of my life, on perfect course for 2:07:38." Some reporters construed that as predicting a world record—thirty-five seconds under Salazar's mark—but Dixon said he was only describing the shape he was in.

Patterson, forty-eight, still a solid 190 pounds twenty years after being heavyweight champion, had run three marathons, his latest being a very respectable 3:40. The difference between running and fighting, he said, was that "in running, if I get tired, I'll stop; in boxing, if you get tired and stop, you'll get murdered."

Patricia Owens, a former executive with New York's Off-Track Betting Corporation, was immersed in arrangements for invited runners and VIPs—money, travel, hotels, special requests. For 1983 the general standard for runners to be invited under the "elite" category (to receive all expenses and a per diem) was that American men must have run a 2:14 marathon within the last two years, American women a 2:40; foreign men a 2:12, women a 2:35. For other invited runners (just under the "elite" category, and excluding celebrities), who are guaranteed nothing except entry, the standard (with some flexibility) is 2:30 for men and 3:00 for women; any of those men, however, who subsequently run here in 2:16 or better, or women who run 2:42 or better, are reimbursed for expenses. Among the VIPs observing this year's race would be fifty marathon directors from around the world, including the director of the 1984 Olympic marathons.

Controller Bob Miller, who left a prestigious accounting firm to join us a year before, expanded his three-person staff temporarily to about ten to handle marathon finances. (Originally, when he saw how we handled money at marathon time—thousands of dollars of loose cash floating around for the requirements and requests of elite runners and so on—Bob was so upset over lax accounting procedures that he almost resigned. I told him that our way was necessary, practical, and not dishonest. He checked with his former firm, and they said it wasn't a serious problem. So while he established an efficient accounting system of high standards for us, Bob learned to be flexible.)

Our foreign athletes' liaison, Terpsie Toon (a stage dancer and actress), was plowing through the entries of noninvited foreigners, most of them with tour groups, and entering their data into the computer. Foreign athletes constitute about a quarter of our field. We have quotas where necessary—about 850 from England, for example, the largest delegation. Next largest is France, then Italy. Sixty-eight nations would be represented in 1983, up six from the previous year.

Brian Caulfield, editor of our *New York Running News,* was tucking in the last-minute changes and additions in our marathon-program edition (145 pages, including the complete entry list).

TAC Executive Director Ollan Cassell came to town, and TAC lawyer Chriss wanted to put him and me together to help heal the rift. I wouldn't go to Cassell's turf—the New York Athletic Club. And Cassell wouldn't come to my turf—the New York Road Runners Club. We met on a bench in Central Park. At first we bickered over our respective roles in the sport. As far as our club is concerned, I said, "What's good for the sport is good for us." Cassell said my true attitude was, "What's good for Fred Lebow is good for the sport." But we were able to chat for a while and ease hostilities. I agreed to keep him better informed on what we were up to.

Bill Noel, our course and start coordinator, was seeing to everything, from the ordering of 320 portable toilets to the paving of potholes in the road, along with organizing the staging area at Fort Wadsworth. Under him, Bob Merolla, a professional mason who takes care of heavy logistics and drives our black Ford pickup, equipped with radios, loudspeakers, and flashing dome lights and customized for heavy duty to haul our construction-type command trailer around, was tracing and retracing the course with Transportation Department ombudsman Sam Azadian, marking and logging in all sorts of obstructions that would need attention.

A long stretch of First Avenue in Manhattan would be repaved in time for the marathon. Carpets would be laid on four bridges this year instead of two, installation set for the day before the race. We had ordered $10,000 worth of painted metal mileage markers, which would be strapped to light poles along the course, and twenty thousand No Parking signs (four times what we needed, to allow for pilferage as souvenirs) printed this year, not only in English but in Spanish and Yiddish as well, for use in those ethnic neighborhoods.

Steve Mendelsohn, our ham-radio coordinator, was drawing together his network of more than two hundred operators—a team that has grown to become the largest nonemergency amateur network for any event anywhere. They were the vital nerve center for the race, tying together everybody—officials and police—with communications. Major radio centers would be set up at the start and finish. Operators would be spaced at every quarter mile along the course, and at least one would be assigned to accompany every senior race official on race day.

Medical Director Dr. Andres Rodriguez, an orthopedic surgeon at Methodist Hospital in Brooklyn, was organizing and training our corps of 1,500 medical personnel (doctors, nurses, paramedics), who would be stationed at every mile along the course and at the finish. The U.S. Army Reserve's 74th Field Hospital would provide tents and 250 trained reservists to attend to injured or sick runners at the finish. Consolidated Edison personnel would, as always, distribute tables, cups, and other material to water and aid stations along the course. Pan American World Airways joined us as a sponsor. They would provide 186 free seats for travel, and we could use them either to bring in invited runners or for members of our staff. Xerox sponsored the twenty thousand silver Mylar blankets given to finishers.

The Buick people wanted to fly a hot-air balloon near the finish line in Central Park. I told them not even to ask—Parks wouldn't consider it. Then they thought maybe they could fly it over the staging area at Fort Wadsworth.

Security coordinator Jerry Klasman (who supervised a technical-writing department at a bank) was holding instructional meetings with his race crew, which had heaviest responsibility for control of the finish-line area, and was setting up systems with an expert team from Columbia Presbyterian Medical Center, which would provide our security for registration and the Marathon Exposition at the hotel. Jerry was also in charge of producing and distributing the various types of credentials, each color-coded and printed to allow access to a specific area. The press alone would get more than two thousand credentials. The most coveted credential was, of course, the All-Area one given to certain senior staff; that one included a photograph of the wearer laminated under plastic.

Volunteer coordinator Jolene Roberts was so overwhelmed with day and night telephoning to organize 4,500 volunteers that, even though she had recently married, more often than not she slept on a cot in her office.

Clay Smith, our merchandising manager, had worked out a deal with Macy's and Bloomingdale's to sell our T-shirts and sweat shirts during Marathon Week—the first time we had sold our gear through another company. The competition for our official marathon T-shirt design had been narrowed down to the final few submissions, and I picked an Art Deco design that few others liked.

The woman we hire to produce our parties, Mickey Mizrachy, was finalizing plans for the disco party at the Sheraton Centre. Live music, special lighting, a fashion show, and all the rest would cost around $6,500. I also wanted her to arrange for six street-wide arches of balloons to fly over the course and to order roses for all the female finishers (my idea borrowed from Berlin).

Muriel Frohman, a volunteer upon whom we rely for matters involving elegance and taste, was arranging for trophies.

ABC had come up with a new vehicle for our race: a motorcycle with back-to-back seats, the cameraman facing backward. This would give them a more mobile camera position to move back and forth along the field of runners. The telecast this year would be carried in thirteen other countries: Japan, Ecuador, New Zealand, Canada, Denmark, West Germany, Iceland, Holland, Korea, England, Jamaica, Trinidad, and Peru.

Our media director, Gloria Averbuch, who would be the race commentator on WABC radio, was preparing to broadcast daily marathon reports leading up to the day of the race. WABC was planning to hand out 100,000 tiny flags to spectators along the course.

Even so mundane a matter as planning the lunch packets for the runners involved discussions. Del Monte wanted a more significant mention in the program because, unlike other things in the packets, their bananas had no company name on them. The company that would provide twenty thousand individually packaged frozen bagels intended to charge us two thousand dollars to cover their cost. I told them they were shortsighted because if they charged us they couldn't be thanked in the program and ads as contributors. They charged us anyway.

Appeals letters were pouring in from rejected applicants who were begging to be let in for one reason or another: The mail got fouled up; entry blanks got lost; running partners or spouses got accepted but the writers didn't. There were appeals for physical-health reasons, mental-health reasons, love reasons.

A married woman in New Mexico wrote that she had fallen in love with a married man at a running camp; they were desperate to run our marathon together in order to spend time with each other; she was feeling suicidal, this might save her life.

A nun asked for acceptance because running was a good way to be "in touch with the Lord," and the New York City Marathon was the most profound place to run.

An inmate of a New York State prison begged for entry because he had been training in prison and would be released just in time to run New York. A Florida prisoner wanted to run "by proxy" in his prison yard if I would assign him a number and include him in the official results.

Lots of people plead that they deserve a chance because they have been turned down several times already. One guy from New York City asked for acceptance because he had been turned down three straight times. But then he went on to charge us with being a "clique" that didn't accept him because he wasn't part of the "pecking order." That went in the wastebasket.

Most of the letters are handled routinely by Alice Schneider and June Haskin (who works on registration, and with Alice on computer operations). They received a particularly poignant letter: A young man wrote that his older brother had run the New York City Marathon as one of his final acts before dying of cancer. The man had kept his brother's running shoes. Now he himself wanted to be accepted "to run in my dead brother's shoes."

The trouble was, Alice remembered receiving the same plea from the same guy the year before. We bought it once, but not twice.

A man called to yell at me because we hadn't accepted a one-legged boy he had asked us to take. I told him that the reason the boy hadn't been accepted was that he had never been entered through the proper channels, as had other handicapped runners, including three amputees we had accepted. The man threatened to take the matter to the press. "That just shows what kind of guy you are," I said, "to try and make us look like bad guys when the fact is you never took the trouble to enter your young friend." Having promised the boy he would get in, the man now didn't know what to tell him. "Tell him the truth," I said, "that you didn't apply for him until it was too late, and if you do it properly next year, we'll probably accept him."

Celebrities wanted in. Former Miss America Kylene Barker-Brandon wrote asking for an invitation so she could be the first Miss America to run our marathon. Shawn Weatherly, Miss Universe of 1980, asked for an invitation. Billy Mills, the half-Indian who in 1964 became the only American ever to win an Olympic gold medal in the 10,000 meters and was now the subject of a movie called *Running Brave,* sent a list of people he hoped we could accept, including Robbie Benson, who plays him in the movie. Barbie Benton, the country singer and former *Playboy* centerfold, appealed for acceptance of her husband. Robert Earl Jones, the father of actor James Earl Jones, called to request acceptance. He had been the oldest entrant in our 1976 marathon and was now nearly eighty. He assured me he was in shape, and I asked him to come in to see me. I wanted to look him over. Within an hour he arrived—tall, courtly, gracious, with the same booming voice as his son—wearing our 1976 marathon medal around his neck. How could I resist? I recommended a special entry for him. We also accepted superstar skier Jean-Claude Killy, who won three gold medals in the 1968 Winter Olympics, and Julie Ridge, an actress who had achieved fame in 1983 for becoming the first person ever to swim twice around Manhattan (fifty-six miles)—both first-time marathoners.

Cunard Lines called to say the *Queen Elizabeth* 2 would arrive in New York early on the morning of the marathon and four of the ship's officers who had been training on board (including during the ship's wartime trip to the Falkland Islands) wanted to run our marathon for the first time. But to make it to the start, they could not wait for the ship to go all the way in to the Manhattan dock; they would have to be let off in the Narrows near the Verrazano Bridge and take a launch to shore on Staten Island. I agreed to cooperate.

Television crews came in almost daily for interviews, including a crew from England making a documentary on marathons. WNBC did a series on the marathon; WABC produced a special to run just before the race. A reporter from *Life* magazine picked my brains about the favorites to win the Olympic marathons. A writer from *Forbes* interviewed me about finances. Reporters from *The New York Times* and Long Island's *Newsday* were also working on articles about money. Since 1980, major publications, such as the *Washington Post* and *The New York Times*, had been publishing stories speculating (pretty accurately) about how much under-the-table prize money we were paying. Now with other marathons paying money openly and legally, I was not as comfortable this year in hedging about it or being coy. Maybe, I dared hope once again, by next year the mayor would come around.

Two weeks before the marathon we painted the blue line. It's one responsibility I never delegate to anyone else. Even though it's been done by the same Highway Department crew for eight years, I am always afraid something could go wrong. The first night we painted in Queens and Brooklyn, the second night Manhattan. Always when we have started to paint in Manhattan, we have been met by a lot of press and hoopla. This time there was nobody—maybe it was getting to be old hat. But in Central Park we were picked up by a local WABC-TV crew, then by an ABC network crew. To pacify the Parks Department, in Central Park we painted the line in shorter, thinner dashes so automobile tires would more quickly erase it after the marathon.

For weeks Allan and TAC's Chriss had been working to put

together a prize-money arrangement that would allow us to be competitive with other marathons while protecting us from appearing to be overcommercial—an application for a TACTRUST sanction that would be legal but not publicized.

No sooner had they produced a final document satisfying to everybody than Chriss stormed into my office, irate. He had seen an advance copy of the *Forbes* magazine article about me and our finances, and he accused me of violating our mutual agreement to keep quiet about prize money. All I had told *Forbes* was that we couldn't give open prize money this year because it might give the Russians and East Europeans an excuse to boycott the Olympics—about the same thing I had said earlier in Helsinki. The article had gone on to point out that TAC was giving sanctions for prize-money marathons like Chicago. Chriss was fuming because I had agreed not to say anything that would make TAC "the whipping boy," and now he felt that I had implied that I was more concerned than TAC was about rules and Russians and the Olympics. He said my comments in the article "made TAC sound like the rat and Fred Lebow the protector of athletes in America." I would have to be more careful in future interviews.

Our second floor, ordinarily busy with clinics, exercise classes, and especially these days with marathon-organization meetings, was taken over by an art show, "Marathon '83," featuring high-priced paintings and sculptures on the theme of running. It was curated by my assistant, Debbie Ulian, a former art-history student at Yale (and captain of the Yale women's cross-country team), and artist-runner Art Guerra. Some of the staff were irked to have an art show get in the way of marathon business, but I thought it would add a classy dimension and draw some important visitors to the club. A crowd of maybe six hundred jammed in for the opening-night party, and it became a Bohemian zoo. I found three guys smoking pot on the back stairs and threw them out. Art Guerra brought them back in, explaining that they were three of the top graffiti artists in the country.

Other club events continued as scheduled, including one that gave us particular pride. Inside the razor-wire fences of the city's maximum-security prison on Riker's Island in the East River, we staged the first Riker's Island Olympics, a track meet for male and female prisoners. It was directed by Milena Krondl, who also heads our Urban Running Program. (Milena, one of our most valuable hands, especially in the areas that get the least press attention, is a Czechoslovakian who arrived in the United States in 1968 as a makeup person with a touring Czech theater. She was in San Antonio when the Russians invaded her country. She stayed in this country, doing odd jobs and learning English, found her way to New York City in 1970, and came to work with us a couple of years ago.) Mayor Koch fired the starter's pistol for the opening sprint event.

We got another unwelcomed shot of publicity about money: *Newsday* published an article revealing more details than anyone else had about our current prize-money problems. It said that Mayor Koch had prohibited prize money and quoted Parks Commissioner Henry Stern as saying: "If the marathon were to give substantial prizes, they would have to run it elsewhere." It also had Alvin Chriss saying that we were in the process of supplying him with a prize-money structure that would show a total purse of something less than $200,000.

Allan thought the article could be disastrous because it put the mayor and the parks commissioner on record as prohibiting prize money at the same time as Chriss seemed to be acknowledging that we were giving it (my comeuppance, I guess, for breaking our agreement). I was less disturbed. Since it was a regional newspaper, it might just blow over. Our luck held. No other reporters followed up on it, and there was no official reaction. It did just blow over.

Problems started to mushroom. There were small ones—such as all five of our copying machines suddenly breaking down at once. And bigger ones. The seven thousand T-shirts to be worn as identification by volunteers and officials had not arrived—they were already two weeks overdue. The bleachers had been positioned wrong in Central Park, and some of the sections had to be torn down and moved. The customization of the Buick lead cars (removing the rear seats, installing roll bars, putting on special vertical tail-pipe extensions that carried exhaust fumes six feet up at the rear to keep them from blowing in the runners' faces) was late; the cars hadn't been delivered. Allan and his right-hand man in electronic and other technical matters, Phil Greenwald, a computer programmer, were working through the bureaucracy of the phone company to get the extensive system of lines (including the data line direct to the *Daily News,* which produces a pullout section of results the morning after) installed in our trailers in Central Park. The installation was already several days late; it was putting us in a real bind because we already had people working in the trailers, and our only communications were by radio.

On top of all that, gremlins struck at the heart of our newest sophistication: the laser printing system that would print runners' numbers in six seconds on the spot as they registered.

Accepted runners had received an I.D. card bar-coded with all relevant information. At registration the card would be inserted into the machinery, and the laser printer (there would be eight printers, furnished by Quality Micro Systems, Inc.) would instantly produce a printed number to be pinned to the runner's shirt. Attached to that number, with perforations to allow easy removal, were the bus tag (for the ride to the start), the baggage tag, tickets to the pasta and disco parties, and the bar-coded duplicate number, to be removed by the scorers at the finish.

But now, in testing the system, Alice Schneider discovered that the printers weren't working on the perforated sheets: Apparently, the perforations were causing the material to jam the machines. If that couldn't be corrected, we would have to do the printing on unperforated sheets and make the perforations afterward by hand. Such a procedure would cause countless hours of backup at registration and make a shambles of our much-promoted high-tech efficiency. But we had no choice; we had to prepare for the worst.

While we contacted company technicians to try to correct the problem within the printers, several of our people began devising imaginative backup systems for manually perforating the sheets. We considered making various jigs—wood frames in which nails or needles or even hacksaw blades or razor blades could be embedded that would make perforations when the printed sheets were pressed down on them. If none of that worked, we might even have to resort to using ordinary paper cutters or round-bladed pizza cutters to slice off the tags and tickets after the numbers were printed at registration.

On October 16, one week before the marathon, we held our 5-mile Computer Run in Central Park to test the scoring system under actual race conditions. The Qantel system, along with hand-held bar-code scanners, produced by Computer Identics, worked fine.

But Allan was still beleaguered by all the other problems and the omens of things to come. "We've never had so many screw-ups as this year," he said.

On that note we moved our marathon headquarters from the NYRRC to the Sheraton Centre Hotel for Marathon Week.

12

Along with truckloads of merchandise and paraphernalia for registration and offices, about fifty of our staff and key volunteers moved into the hotel for the week. We had two days to get ready for opening at noon on Wednesday, when we would begin registering seventeen thousand runners for next Sunday's race.

It was a rocky start. The cavernous Albert Hall exhibition area was a shambles. Nobody had cleaned up after the last occupants, and junk was strewn and piled everywhere. Then a pipe burst, flooding part of the hall. Then there was a bomb threat, called in by a runner who said we had rejected him from the marathon.

The staff, under the direction of Larry Wydro, a former social worker who was one of our race directors, worked to beat the clock. The seventy-five booths of the Marathon Expo, where companies would exhibit their running-related products, took up half the hall. The electronic gear was set up in the registration area. Volunteers stuffed plastic bags for the runners' packets—T-shirts, shorts, informational materials. Wares for the store were displayed on tables, in glass cases, on hangers. International flags went up overhead, posters and signs went up on the walls. Telephone lines went in. Staff offices were a few curtained cubicles off the registration area.

Before 9 A.M. on Wednesday the first registrants were standing in a line that reached outside the hotel. We still didn't know if the laser printers would work. But that morning we received a new supply of different printing stock; the printers tested perfectly.

At noon security people at the door began letting in groups of runners to go through registration (only runners with marathon I.D.s and other credentialed people, such as club officials, people manning Expo booths, and press, were allowed into the hall). Staff members were stationed everywhere to direct people into proper lines, answer questions. The new printers produced each bib number with its attached tags in just six seconds, then each newly printed number was subject to an exit check; an electronic scanner was passed over the bar code to assure that it was a proper number. At the end of the row of registration counters was the "Trouble Desk." Anyone whose number didn't clear or who had some other problem that interfered with registration went to the Trouble Desk, where their entries could be looked up on the computer sheets. Entrants from France had a lot of problems because there had been a postal strike in Paris. As a result, many French entry I.D.s were lost or delayed.

Once the runners had their numbers, they went to the end of the hall to pick up their packets; then they were free to visit the store and Expo.

Although the wait to register was seldom more than an hour, daily the line extended outside the hotel and halfway around the block. Inside the hotel security was excellent. Our guards, communicating with each other and us by walkie-talkie, even slit open some of the trash bags before they were hauled away to make sure no merchandise or equipment was being smuggled out. Outside, though, rip-off artists and hucksters were at work. Some stores were selling T-shirts printed with "Training for the New York Marathon," a violation of our copyright. Peddlers were charging two dollars for caps with the legend "New York Marathon," similar to what we were selling inside. We tried to protect people in the line from being bothered by peddlers and pamphleteers. Usually, when we went after them, they would just melt away into the crowd. Several times I tried to chase one guy who was handing out brochures advertising running gear. Finally I hollered at him, "I told you nicely to stop! Now I'm going to get some strong-armed guys!" "Don't you threaten me!" he hollered back. "Go ahead and get your strong-armed guys!"

There wasn't much we could do since these people were on public property.

The entire midtown area seemed alive with marathoners, and among them, especially around our hotel, lurked the would-be runners with last-minute appeals. As I was walking along the registration line in front of the hotel, a guy wearing a priest's collar approached me. He identified himself as Father Joseph and said he had been accepted for the marathon, and sent in his ten dollars but never received his entry card. He was running, he said, to publicize a particular children's cause. I asked him for any evidence of acceptance, such as a canceled check. He had none. I kept walking. "Sorry," I said, "I can't do anything." He followed me, talking about the poor children. "Maybe next year," I said. I wasn't hardhearted, but there is almost nothing I haven't heard in the way of angles.

Progress was excellent. In the first two days we registered eight thousand runners, more than half the total.

Things were going so well that I allowed myself, for the first time ever, to be taken away from Marathon Week business. Rob Ingraham, of Capital Sports, had lined up CBS to cover our proposed 1984 New York Triathalon, and now he wanted me to make my pitch to General Foods for sponsorship. He drove me up to their headquarters in suburban White Plains. I made my pitch: a classy event, network TV, and so on. CBS wanted to do a half-hour taped show to run in September, so we wanted to hold the event in late summer. The General Foods executives preferred June, to coincide with their introduction on the market of a new artificially sweetened drink. They would think it over.

I came away regretting that I had killed a whole afternoon of Marathon Week making a pitch that the company would probably not buy—because we wouldn't move the event to early summer. (I was wrong. Later they bought the event for a six-figure sponsorship.)

Back at marathon headquarters there were a million things to do. Allan spent much of his time in our trailers at the finish line in Central Park, supervising the fitting together of all the systems, from the electronic to the physical. The actual finish-line complex, with its scaffolding and photographers' platforms and clocks and flags that straddle the park roadway, could not be erected until Saturday, the day before the race, so as not to block the road to traffic. But there was a lot of other hauling and hammering and sign-painting and assembling of equipment to be done. Our people who do the heavy work have adopted the name of "Marathon Grunts," and they wear special jackets so inscribed; Allan has always proudly numbered himself among them, as opposed to those who deal primarily with elite runners and the press.

A crucial job during the week was to promote the race. Among other things, this included appearances at places like Macy's and Bloomingdale's department stores, which were hosting week-long series of visits by running personalities, such as Grete Waitz, Jim Fixx, Bill Rodgers, Eamonn Coghlan. We held daily press conferences, emceed by Stan Saplin, a noted track and field writer and consultant to us, to introduce runners.

Enormous publicity surrounds everything we do that week, from registration to runners. This year we had a tough time. We had taken a lot of flak about prize money and the challenge from Chicago. Four-time New York winner Bill Rodgers, and this year's Boston winner, Greg Meyer, had both opted to run Chicago's open-prize-money marathon held the previous week—Meyer doubting that we could match Chicago's field and saying that "the New York Marathon will try to bail out with gimmicks." New Zealand's Anne Audain, who had beaten Grete Waitz this year in our L'eggs Mini Marathon, also ran Chicago. (Meyer finished fourteenth, Rodgers twenty-seventh; Audain was fourth woman. Joseph Nzau, of Kenya, was the $20,000 winner in a time of 2:09:44.)

The fact is, we were hard pressed to find anything to crow about. Our defending champion, three-time winner Alberto Salazar, was injured. So was Rodolfo Gomez, of Mexico, who had dueled so dramatically with Salazar last year. So was Portugal's

Carlos Lopes, who had been a big hope after his strong showing in Rotterdam. Top-ranked Rob de Castella, of Australia, was not going to run a fall marathon. Neither was world-record holder Joan Benoit. Second best American Julie Brown and New Zealand's Allison Roe, who shared the world record with Grete Waitz before Benoit took it, were injured.

With no household names except Grete Waitz, we lacked our usual star show, and there were smirks in some quarters about us being all hype and no heroes in 1983. I did my best to stress a positive theme: After the world records of 1981 and the spectacular Salazar-Gomez duel of 1982, we would have the new excitement of a truly open competition in 1983. The lack of stars, I pointed out, would create an opportunity for the emergence of new stars; our "people's race" would bring out the very best in some new names and produce some terrific surprises.

I had a hunch about Dixon. Not only did he have a victory in his only marathon to date and his subsequent nineteen-race winning streak, but he had been training obsessively for our marathon since July—treating it, he said, "like a world championship, an Olympic Games." I went out on a limb by predicting not only that Dixon would win but that it would be in the superb time of 2:08:58—which would be the best time in the world since the Rotterdam Marathon in April.

Besides Dixon, there was a bunch of men with the capability to produce heroics, given the added spur of a wide-open field and a chance to win New York. The fastest marathoner in the field, in fact, was an Englishman, John Graham, who, after a third-place finish in the 1980 New York, won the 1981 Rotterdam Marathon in 2:09:28 (faster than Chicago's 1983 winning time). Ron Tabb had become the fifth fastest American marathoner in history with a 2:09:31 second place in this year's Boston, and had gone on to win marathons in Sydney, Australia, and Peking, China. Kevin Ryan, a New Zealander living in Boston, was a two-time Olympian who had won our 25-K Marathon Tune-Up three weeks earlier, and set a new course record in the process. One of the most feared by other runners was Gidamis Shahanga, a Texas college student from Tanzania, who was current NCAA champion at both 5-K and 10-K, and was impressing a lot of people with his training speeds at greater distances. American Paul Cummings had set a world half-marathon record in September with a 1:01:32. And the man who finished right behind Cummings in that race had been Geoff Smith, a twenty-nine-year-old Englishman, one of the top 10-K and 10-milers in the world, but who had never run a marathon—a real dark horse for our race.

For the women, Grete, of course, was in a class by herself if she stayed healthy. Without Benoit and Roe, seemingly nobody could approach her best time of 2:25:29. But we did have New Zealand's Lorraine Moller, who had won a host of international marathons, with a best time of 2:29:35, and who was in her best shape for New York; American Julie Shea, winner of eight collegiate championships and third-place finisher in the 1981 New York; Italy's Alba Milana, who had run a 2:32:57; former world-record holder Christa Vahlensieck, who had run a 2:33:22; and Margaret Groos, American 10-mile record holder (set in our 1983 Trevira Twosome, as Geoff Smith's partner).

I had this strange confidence that in spite of everything we were going to have a great marathon. That was important, because suddenly we were given an opportunity to hedge our bets. The agent who was eventually going to negotiate our new TV contract, Barry Frank, of Trans World International, proposed that he negotiate now, long before our current contract with ABC expired. In fact, he wanted to present to ABC a six-year deal that would begin with a renegotiation of *this year's* contract, and he proposed to do that on Friday, two days before the marathon. He was sure, he said, that he could up this year's price by almost fifty percent, and by 1988 have us getting *800* percent more than the top money in our current contract.

Suddenly, Allan and I found ourselves sitting in our curtained cubicle during registration for the 1983 marathon, confronted by a monumental decision that we would have to make within a few hours. If our agent could sell this deal to ABC, it would change the whole face of our organization; we could be on easy street, with all the flexibility and opportunities that we had dreamed of.

Allan thought wistfully aloud of what miracles this kind of money could perform for the inadequate salaries at our club.

For the 1982 marathon we had drawn a Nielsen rating of 6.8, a 26 percent share of the audience. We had been the highest-rated sports show of the day. But that had been during the NFL football players' strike; nobody could be sure how we would do with the NFL back in the picture. Sports in general were down in the ratings lately. If we were to get poor ratings this year, we would wish that we had taken the agent's proposal and renegotiated ahead of time.

The haste of all this troubled us. But more than that, to renegotiate now, before the marathon, would be to admit lack of confidence in our own show. After discussing it with our lawyer, Bob Laufer, and with Manufacturers Hanover's Charlie McCabe, I said to Allan, "From the very beginning, I have gambled on our marathon, always believing it would be bigger than anybody thought. My instinct is still to gamble. Let's wait."

Allan agreed. We would not negotiate now. We would produce a great race. If the marathon could hold firm in the ratings this weekend, we would be golden.

The wheelchair issue surfaced again. Marty Ball, a member of our Achilles Track Club for handicapped runners, had applied for the marathon. We hadn't committed ourselves. On Thursday, Alice Cashman, of the Parks Department, informed us that Ball's lawyer was insisting that he be allowed to race and that Parks Comissioner Henry Stern was also adamant that we admit him. Our board had voted to ask any wheelchair applicants to withdraw, but Ball hadn't withdrawn. Even though the courts had given us the right to bar wheelchairs, we didn't want another confrontation. Instead, we wanted a bargain. Parks had planted a new small tree near the finish line, right where some bleachers were supposed to go. I wanted the tree removed. Cashman said that would cost us a thousand dollars. I got the price down to two hundred. The tree came out, Ball got in. And I threw in another wheelchair entrant for good measure.

In the last couple of days television crews were doing a lot of shooting around the finish line, interviewing elite runners and celebrities such as Jean-Claude Killy. Now, on Friday, they wanted to get some film of me in the newly delivered lead car, the customized white Buick convertible. The person who would drive the car during the race was Judy Woodfin, a Hertz executive. She was irked. Hertz had previously supplied the lead cars, and now Judy was compelled to drive a car that wasn't a Hertz. Furthermore, Hertz had to share the billing with Buick, and on the car doors where there were Hertz signs above Buick signs, Buick wanted the positions reversed to take top billing. "This is too much," Judy said. "It's not even Buick, really, just the New York–New Jersey dealers. And they're appearing to be a full sponsor when they're not. *We're* a sponsor. I'm telling you, if you use Buick next year, you'll lose Hertz."

Right then, I didn't want to lose anybody. Buick had already been officially rejected in its proposal to fly a hot-air balloon over Fort Wadsworth or the Verrazano Bridge. But for Hertz's sake, we at least kept the door signs the way they were.

Saturday. The last day of registration. By nighttime all the booths, rigging, merchandise, machinery would be cleared from Albert Hall. The finish-line structure would be up. The Army Reserves would have rolled into Central Park with their big olive-drab trucks and generators and hospital tents. There would be no sleep from now until long after tomorrow's marathon, after the awards ceremony, after the disco party.

The day began at 8 A.M. with the gathering of foreign runners at the United Nations Plaza for our annual Manufacturers Hanover International Breakfast Run. Before the assembled mass of four thousand marathoners from sixty-eight countries, grouped under their national flags, we presented our fifth annual Abebe Bikila Award for outstanding contributions to long-distance running. Abebe Bikila was the Ethiopian marathoner who set world records in winning the Olympic gold medals in 1960 and 1964. In 1969 he was paralyzed from an automobile accident, and he died four years later. Our previous winners had been Emil Zatopek, of Czechoslovakia, Lasse Viren, of Finland, Mamo

Walde, of Ethiopia, and American Frank Shorter. We presented the 1983 award to our first woman recipient, Grete Waitz.

Then, with a police escort, the international field of marathon entrants, carrying their countries' flags, jogged two miles through city streets to Tavern-on-the-Green in Central Park for a festive breakfast.

A couple hundred yards from the restaurant on the Park Drive, workers were erecting the huge photographers' bridge, a scaffolding of metal tubing and wooden platforms used just for this event. Twenty yards in front of that, at the finish line itself, finish-line director David Pearlman (an eight-year veteran at this job, and dean of students at the high school where Allan once taught and coached track) and his team of Grunts were assembling the structure under which the finishers would cross the line and on which would be mounted the clocks and banner; a custom-made system of metal sections resembling extension ladders, designed for us by a man who does work for NASA.

All week long in our marathon headquarters the phones in our cubicles never stopped ringing. Workers, sponsors, city officials—everybody—kept calling or coming in looking for Allan or me (we were supposed to be reachable at any time, anywhere, via the beepers we wore on our belts, but I usually forgot to turn mine on) or asking for things: extra party tickets, special credentials, official rain gear, and other favors. My assistant, Debbie Ulian, was preoccupied in a hotel suite matching clothes to models for the disco-party fashion show. So most of the hassles in the office fell to Allan's overworked but unflappable and unfailingly pleasant assistant, Mamie Phillips.

The night before the marathon more than six thousand runners gathered to be seated in shifts in the dining room at the Manufacturers Hanover Trust Company headquarters on Park Avenue for the traditional marathon-eve pasta party. They were greeted by a brass band and people dressed up in Moosehead moose costumes. They ate limitless spaghetti and drank limitless bottles of Moosehead beer and Perrier water.

Later I went to the finish line. The finish line on the night before the marathon is like no other sight. Although we have crews there working under the floodlights, it is a place of serenity and silence compared to what we have been through in the weeks before. Tomorrow it would be a madhouse. So I drank it in.

Although rain was predicted for tomorrow, this night before was clear and cool, with just enough breeze to stir the yellow leaves on the park trees. Empty blue bleachers stretched for hundreds of yards on both sides of the Park Drive up to the finish line. In front of them our new silver metal barricades were a neat interlocking fence that defined the roadway as the runners' turf. Painted blue dashes led to the finish line. Our new banner extended across the road. And over it, anchored to the cross-beams, the big rectangular electronic timing clocks had black faces on which yellow numbers would flash tomorrow when the race started twenty-six miles away. Further on, the two-tiered photographers' bridge towered over the scene. To one side, in the grass beyond the trailers, the big Emergency Medical Services tent glowed orange from inside lights like a Halloween pumpkin. To the other side sat the ABC trailers, with generators humming. Further off, half hidden in the trees—a world away—was Tavern-on-the-Green, where tomorrow we would present our winners to the international press.

Alice Schneider was at work in the computer trailer. In another trailer Allan, Raleigh Mayer, and Jerry Klasman reviewed logistics for trips to the Fort Wadsworth staging area and the start; officials would begin moving over there at 3 A.M. One of the rented vans we would use had a dead battery. Bob Merolla, who would be cruising the course all night and through the race, arrived with our truck to jump-start the van. Outside the trailer freshly painted signs to identify water stations and aid stations along the course were spread out to dry. David Pearlman was dragging into place the concrete stanchions that would anchor the ropes for channeling the runners.

My main job the night before is to put up dozens of international flags and hang our original finish-line banner. I love flags. I want as many as possible flying over our race. I tape their staffs to the highest reaches of the photographers' bridge, the announcer's stand, the bleachers. As a rather private finishing touch, at the center atop the photographers' bridge I put the flags of two nations from which I believe the male and female winners will come. This time it was the flags of New Zealand and Norway.

Our original banner goes on the back of the photographers' bridge, facing the rear, where the chutes and additional photographers will be. I have nostalgic feelings about the tattered old banner. Every year it is more torn, and every year I lay it down on the road and tape the ripped sections.

It was 2 A.M. by the time I finished this task. By 3 A.M. a group of us—Allan, Vince Chiappetta, Larry Wydro, Patricia Owens, Bill Noel, Steve Mendelsohn and some of his ham operators, and a few others—were lounging in the hotel lobby having coffee and doughnuts just before leaving for Fort Wadsworth.

"We're going to have three hams in the press photographers' truck," Mendelsohn said to me.

"What are you talking about?" I said. The big, open Sanitation Department truck, with platforms installed in the back to provide different elevations, was always jammed with photographers. "It's been two for the last seven years. And with all the photographers that are begging for places, you're going to give that to a *ham*? I don't believe it. You can't do it."

"I *am* doing it," Mendelsohn said. "I wish you would ride in that truck just once and see what it's like. We need a guy in the cab with the driver, and a guy in the back talking to him, and another to talk to me in the lead car and deal with the photographers, who are always yelling and screaming about where they want the truck to be. It's essential to have three."

We started shouting back and forth until Allan interceded. "Will you two guys shut up right now! You usually don't start this until four o'clock."

We piled into vans and station wagons for the trip to Fort Wadsworth. Allan and I always ride in separate vehicles for such trips—like the President and Vice President—so that if anything happens to the vehicle carrying one of us, the other at least will get there. After the start of the race Allan is delivered directly back to the finish line with a police escort.

Except for the guards at the gate, Fort Wadsworth was dark and quiet. We set up headquarters in the building housing the gymnasium. Mendelsohn and his radio people began checking and adjusting their equipment. Allan set up his own command station. He would maintain radio communications with the ham network and would have direct phone lines to people at the finish line. Some of the hams would stay in the building, others would fan out over the staging area and start. Mendelsohn would dog my footsteps with his radio—something he calls "an art acquired over the years" because I am moving all the time in unpredictable directions to check everything. Mendelsohn would relay messages to and from me. And dogging *his* footsteps was an attractive young woman with another radio (a former Miss Alaska, Mendelsohn said) whom he was breaking in on the job of learning to follow me around.

On the grass fields of the staging area the Red Cross was already set up with piles of packaged rolls and big metal urns of coffee and hot chocolate. Huge tents were ready to house runners who wanted to relax out of the elements. The check-in area, where arriving runners would have their bar-coded bib numbers read by hand-held electronic scanners, was under an open-sided tent, which provided the necessary shade and protection for the scanners.

At the rear of the fort, closest to the bridge, we cut through the chain link fence and peeled it back to create a wide gate through which arriving runners could enter the fort, and everybody could exit when it was time to go to the start.

We went up on the bridge. It was the warmest morning I could remember for this time, low 50s, cloudy but so far dry. The first red of dawn showed over Brooklyn at the far end of the bridge. Traffic was moving through some of the toll booths to the lower level. We darted through the traffic to the building housing the Triboro Bridge and Tunnel Authority. I was looking for the barricades that would be used at the start. We could find only fifteen of them and we needed sixty!

The lieutenant in charge said he expected more to arrive soon from Brooklyn, but he didn't know how many, or when. For the start, all the toll plazas would be closed, and the barricades set up to funnel the runners from the wider plazas down to the two eight-lane sections of each side of the bridge: One side is the "Blue Start" for veteran men, the other is the "Red Start" for all women and for first-time men. The Red Start is a couple hundred yards farther up the bridge from the Blue Start; the two sides run exactly the same distance but don't merge until about eight miles into the race.

The barricades are crucial for an orderly start, and we use them the same way every year. But every year we go through this same frustrating confusion over how many barricades we are supposed to have and where they are supposed to go. We set up what few barricades we had in the roadway.

On the center divider technicians were setting up the mammoth multitiered speakers of the sound system that would broadcast music and instructions over the whole starting area; it was connected to another sound system within the fort to communicate with the runners beforehand.

The pace signs—minutes per mile painted on cardboard nailed to wooden staffs—would be spaced along the two starts to guide runners where to line up, in descending order of expected running speed. Last year we had people hold the signs. This year we tried planting them in traffic cones. The wind came up. The signs were blown over. We tried nailing the staffs to the barricades. The wind whipped the signs, but I hoped they would hold.

Allan radioed that there was confusion about how to set up the pressroom at Tavern-on-the-Green; the raised platforms for the winners and attending officials were not being installed where I had directed. I insisted it had to be done as ordered.

Shortly after 5:30 the first of 150 buses carrying runners arrived from Lincoln Center in Manhattan. They unloaded near the toll plaza, and the runners walked up along a path in the gulley and through our opening in the fence into the fort. Others quickly followed, and so did a swarm of private cars, all disgorging runners.

But unauthorized people were getting into the fort, too—friends, curious onlookers. M.P.s supposed to be guarding both our entrance and the front gate weren't there. We put out calls for our own marshals to man the gates.

Under the check-in tent the scanners were working fine as the lines of runners passed through. But some of the bar codes were falling off; the perforations were too wide. It would be a disaster for runners to lose their bar codes before they went through the scoring at the finish. Mendelsohn radioed for Scotch tape; we would have to tape on every loose bar code.

Pace signs were blowing over, taking the barricades with them. There was nothing to do but keep standing them back up. The first raindrops fell. Paint on the signs began to run. Between the wind blowing them over and the numbers bleeding into long streaks, the signs were almost useless.

The howitzer arrived on the back of a flatbed truck, and the young soldiers in dress uniforms maneuvered it into place.

It was almost 9 A.M. One more trip inside the fort. The gates were still understaffed, and security was lax. By now it was too late to worry about it. On the roof of a low building our exercise team was leading hundreds of runners down below in calesthenics. The portable toilets were running out of paper. The elite runners were late; the police escort hadn't arrived to lead the buses from Manhattan. Check-in was proceeding, bar codes were being taped.

Mendelsohn had to leave me temporarily for an urgent problem with radios back in the gymnasium building. Miss Alaska stayed on my heels with her radio. I had a less urgent call. I had to visit the "world's longest urinal"—a one-hundred-foot-long trough we put up every year. Miss Alaska turned her head away to wait. When I left the trough, she was no longer with me. I couldn't spend time looking for her. I would do without a radio until she or Mendelsohn caught up.

The elite runners finally arrived at 9:30. The whole field of runners was now present, swarming around the fort grounds in nervous anticipation.

I left the fort for the final time. I would stay on the bridge now until the start. Spectators had begun to gather. They were all over the place. We got a few more barricades—not nearly enough—and set them up.

Bob Merolla radioed in from Brooklyn that the barricades to divide Fourth Avenue, maintaining the separation of the Red and Blue sides as they come off the bridge, were not in place. There were several minutes of panic. But as Bob drove on up the route in the truck, he found that the barricades were going up from the other direction.

Press people were buzzing around looking for last-minute interviews. Bill Rodgers and Kathy Switzer were huddled under umbrellas, giving commentary to a TV camera; they would ride in the ABC camera cars, Rodgers covering the male racers, Switzer the women. Photographers and TV cameras were stationed on the very tops of the bridge stanchions, hundreds of feet up from the roadway. Overhead, maybe a dozen helicopters hovered, including four from ABC and some from the Police Department.

The lead vehicles assembled for both starts—police cars, tow trucks, our lead cars, photographers' trucks, Hertz airport buses for reporters, timing cars with the Seiko digital clocks mounted on the roofs, ABC camera cars. The police motorcycle escorts roared into place.

At 10:00 Mendelsohn got word that the sound system in the fort had gone out—just when announcements were beginning to be made to the runners about depositing their baggage and getting ready to move out. There were some signs of panic—runners were afraid they were missing announcements to go to the start.

All bridge traffic was now stopped. At 10:25 I passed the word to send up the runners. They poured through the rear gate in a stampede. Dozens of our marshals in yellow rain suits tried to herd them into place, but they overwhelmed us. My concern was the front of the pack. Yelling through the bullhorn, I tried to get the elite runners up at the front and the rest back behind them.

Spectators were spilling around the barricades and spreading out onto the bridge. I ran along, begging them to clear the area, warning them that the runners might mow them down.

The mayor was standing on the platform at the howitzer. Next to him, ready to give him the countdown, was Allan, a red phone to his ear with a direct line to the computer trailer at the finish; the finish line would hear the countdown at the same time.

It was time to get into the lead car with Mendelsohn, driver Judy Woodfin, and Charlie McCabe. To my right, across the center divider, the Red Start looked ready—marshals were spread across the front, elite women filled the first rows as they were supposed to, the first-time men were behind them. But directly behind me was a wild scene. At the Blue Start marshals were still trying to muscle everybody back to the line. A few yards up the road from the start, a few policemen were casually milling around in the roadway. "Officers, off the roadway!" I called through the bullhorn. "Please, officers, you're in the way!" They didn't seem to hear me.

Runners were still pouring from the fort, trampling through the shrubbery in a wild, late effort for a shortcut to reach the start in time. Allan gave the command, and the mayor fired the howitzer. Runners were still climbing through the gulley when a puff of smoke came from the howitzer. We were rolling.

We edged away from the pack, our view behind mostly obscured by the press vehicles. As we reached the crest of the bridge, near the one-mile mark, we pulled even with the Red side and the elite women. But then I saw one guy sprinting ahead of the women, in front by thirty yards—some first-time jerk trying to get attention from the TV cameras at the expense of the women. "Get out of there, you stupid idiot!" I bellowed at him with the bullhorn. "You don't belong there! You'll never make it off the bridge!"

Despite the misty rain, the skyline of Manhattan was visible. Way down below, in the waters of the Narrows, a fireboat sprayed streams of red, white, and blue water to celebrate the start.

We came down off the bridge, past the two-mile mark, and swung around to Brooklyn's Fourth Avenue.

The race was well under way now, even the back of the pack cleared of the starting line. Once all the runners are moving, the race has a power and impetus of its own. Allan was on his way to the finish line, where he would key into the computers the official time as shown on his stopwatch and supervise the final preparations to receive the winners two hours from now, and the rest of the field for three hours or more after that. Our job in the lead car is mainly to make sure the course is open ahead of the race. Moving a half mile or more ahead of the leading runners, we could glimpse them only sporadically between the press and timing vehicles which trailed us much closer to the runners. Mendelsohn was busy on his radio, coordinating the movements of the press vehicles at my direction, making sure each got its share of time in the most desired positions. He also kept in touch with other points along the course, and with Bob Merolla, who was cruising far ahead in the truck making sure the course was in order.

We also had a police radio by which we could keep abreast of their messages. The TV monitor mounted in the front of the car, which is usually our best view of the race, was not getting a picture. We were tracking the race mainly by radio.

The motorcycles were ahead of us, behind us, beside us, the riders expertly guiding their wheels inches from the curbs to move spectators back, occasionally using their sirens. They maneuvered in and out among the vehicles to relay messages and give instructions, shouting over the roar of their engines. Lt. Vincent Abbene, their leader, was the main contact with my car.

The crowds were thick, even in the rain, but quiet—they couldn't see the runners yet. "Cheer the runners as they go by!" I urged them.

Mendelsohn said the 10-K time was 29:47—very fast. I was picking up only bits and pieces of the race behind us from the radio. In the first few miles a pack of about half a dozen men had moved out to a lead of about twenty yards. The only top runners among them were Gidamis Shahanga and Finland's Jukka Toivola. Then they were joined by Geoff Smith and Paul Cummings. Among the women, Grete Waitz and Lorraine Moller were leading side by side, with Margaret Groos a few paces behind. Groos dropped back, then Moller. Grete was already the sole leader.

The race merged. Shahanga moved out alone. At ten miles he was fifteen seconds ahead of Smith and Cummings. Rod Dixon, Ron Tabb, and Kevin Ryan were in a group behind them. Grete Waitz, running as always with a pack of men (some use her to set a good pace, some just to be in the TV pictures with her), was a minute ahead of Moller.

We passed through the ethnic neighborhoods of Brooklyn—Scandinavian, Italian, German, Hasidic, Hispanic. Several bands were playing music as we passed. Crowds were enthusiastic, happy. They cheered our car as we came through, and some of them thanked me for a "great race," even though the race itself hadn't yet reached them. Our marshals and volunteers at the water and aid stations were alert and organized and ready.

It was raining harder. We passed the Buick hot-air balloon, anchored on the ground in a parking lot near the course.

Lt. Abbene chugged up beside us to report a problem: Police had found large holes in the grating of the Madison Avenue Bridge, ten miles ahead, where the runners would cross from the Bronx back into Manhattan. We radioed ahead to Merolla to take care of it somehow.

We climbed over the Pulaski Bridge, the halfway point, where we left Brooklyn and headed into Queens. "We made it to Queens!" I called to the crowd, and people cheered and waved and laughed. One group was even watching a portable TV under an umbrella. They called to us that the show was coming in great.

The radio reported that Shahanga passed the halfway mark in 1:03:12—the fastest time we'd ever had at this point. That would project into a 2:06:24 marathon, almost two minutes under the world record, certainly too hot a pace to hold. Shahanga had a reputation for sometimes going out too fast, but still, nobody knew for sure what he was capable of. At the same time, Smith was moving up, now just seven seconds back.

On the Queensboro Bridge heading into Manhattan, near the sixteen-mile mark, I took a close look at the carpeting on the walkway. It looked dark and soggy. I feared that would slow the runners. We passed Linda Down, a cerebral palsy victim on crutches, who was moving well alongside Dick Traum, running on his artificial leg. They started early. Linda had completed the race last year in eleven hours and been invited to the White House.

Coming off the Queensboro Bridge and making the loop under it to head up First Avenue, we came upon John Paul Cruz, a one-legged runner on crutches who had started out at 7:30. Huge crowds awaited us on First Avenue. John Paul answered our cheers and those of the crowd with a broad smile.

Smith had passed Shahanga on the Queensboro Bridge, and now we caught a glimpse of them through the vehicles as they followed us onto First Avenue. Smith had a lead of just a step or two.

The noise along First Avenue was nonstop. Throngs with umbrellas lined both sides of the street; people waved from balconies, windows, rooftops. Sirens wailed as the police eased their motorcycles along the curbs.

We passed under a huge arch of pink, red, and white balloons reaching across the street. For an awful moment it looked as if the photographers standing high in the truck behind us would lose their heads on the wire. But as the front of the truck moved under it, the arch of balloons swung up on the airstream and passed over their ducked heads.

As we moved up First Avenue, we became aware of the real drama forming behind us, virtually out of our sight behind the other vehicles. By seventeen miles Smith had opened a lead of about twenty yards on Shahanga and was running a punishing pace of about 4:30 per mile. Rod Dixon had broken from the next pack and closed to about 120 yards of Shahanga.

I told Judy to step on it—I wanted to check the bridges. We sped up the avenue, leaving the race far behind us. Everything was fine on the Willis Avenue Bridge into the Bronx at the twenty-mile point. We hurried through the Bronx and onto the Madison Avenue Bridge. Bright orange pylons marked the holes in the grating; the runners would be well warned.

We slowed to let the race catch us again, coming down through Harlem. "Let's hear it for Harlem!" I yelled to the spectators, who responded. A line of kids in red berets saluted. "The runners are right behind us!"

As we headed down Fifth Avenue toward Central Park, I called out continually to the crowds and our volunteers: "Get ready for the runners! They're coming right behind us, very fast! Water stations, get ready!"

We heard that at the twenty-mile mark Smith had still been on a pace that would bring him in under 2:07. But Dixon had passed Shahanga and was just thirty seconds behind Smith. Smith, who had never run a marathon, was now into the last six miles, which was brand-new territory. This is where your body resources are about gone and the cruel struggle really begins. Dixon, who had run just one marathon, was closing behind him, perhaps with enough left in him for his famed miler's finishing kick. We were likely to have a hell of a finish.

I kept hollering to the crowds and water stations as we entered Central Park. But I was spent. "I can't take this anymore," I said to Charlie McCabe. Suddenly, I was worried. "Steve," I said to Mendelsohn, "tell Allan about the bar codes, that we had to tape them on, and they might be falling off. Tell him to make provisions for scoring numbers manually, by our regular backup system. Judy," I said to our driver, "let's take off, speed it up and head right for the finish." We took off.

I felt a kind of panic in my weariness. If there was trouble with the timing and scoring at the finish, or difficulties from the rain, there was really not much I could do about it. And we had people there who could deal with any situation. But I felt I had to get there.

"Freddy," Mendelsohn said, turning from his radio and shouting above the wind, "Allan has already made arrangements for manual scoring. They already know, Freddy, they're all set, just waiting."

As we entered Central Park and sped through it, I caught bits of information from the radio: Smith was struggling, his pace slowing; Dixon was gaining—only fourteen seconds behind as they entered the park at the twenty-three-mile point.

At Columbus Circle, a half mile from the finish, we headed north toward the line. The crowds were tremendous, packing the bleachers on both sides and all the spaces in between. They gave us an incredible greeting, umbrellas rocking as they cheered and waved.

They knew as well as we just how dramatically the race was shaping up, as the leaders approached the end. The photographers' bridge was jammed. Officials, security people, timers, and police were everywhere.

Just before the finish line Judy halted the car long enough for us to jump out, and I sprinted for the finish.

There was maybe a minute before the winners would arrive. Finish-line officials were gathered at or behind the line, getting ready with clocks and the tape, which the first runner would break. Allan and I met in front of the line, a few yards down the course. Suddenly cops grabbed us both and tried to wrestle us off the course. We were in a panic; we struggled and yelled who we were. "I don't care who you are," one cop shouted, "our orders are to clear the course!" Allan managed to get the attention of a cop we knew, a lieutenant from the Central Park precinct. He came running over and told the cops holding us that we were indeed the people in charge of the marathon. We were free.

Suddenly, the motorcycles and the leaders appeared. Dixon had passed Smith. Right under the twenty-six-mile banner, 385 yards from the finish, Dixon surged by him and was headed for the line. Allan was ready with one end of the tape, his stopwatch in hand. I was twenty or thirty yards down the course, screaming encouragement at Dixon, waving him wildly on.

He sailed by me as the overhead clocks at the finish line ticked down: 2:08:56, 57, 58 . . .

Dixon threw his arms into the air as he broke the tape: 2:08:59. He dropped to his knees and kissed the asphalt, then raised his arms to the sky. Nine seconds after Dixon, Smith staggered across the line, sank to the road, and rolled over on his back.

Dixon had just run the tenth fastest marathon in history. Smith had run the fastest time ever in the world for a first-time marathon.

Medics helped Smith to his feet. I grabbed Dixon in a hug. Drowned out by the crowd and drenched by the rain, I babbled: "We did it! We did it again!"

13

The story of marathoning so far has been one of dreams and experiments and taking chances, of trial and error, of growth and success in a world of doubts and cynicism. Ordinary people weren't supposed to be able to run marathons—but they did. You couldn't put on a marathon in the heart of a major city—but it was done. You couldn't attract substantial international attention. You couldn't raise enough money. You couldn't make the amateur rules more flexible. All the things that couldn't be done have been shown to be possible. New York City has provided one of the most significant crucibles for the testing of the marathon chemistry, and the theory has been proven.

Whether the New York City Marathon is the premier road race in the world is less important than the fact that we helped pioneer an event that an entire city can take to heart. Other cities around the world are now experiencing what we have. Virtually every major capital in the world now has or soon will have a marathon running through its downtown streets.

We have come to a turning point in the sport. Up to now, our demographics have shown that runners come predominantly from middle-class or upper middle-class professionals. Of the 17,000 entrants in 1983, the largest single group was educators, of which there were 1,075. Then came lawyers (934) and business executives (855), followed by engineers, accountants, physicians, business owners, and bankers.

What we have seen so far is modest compared to the boom that is bound to come as more levels of society participate in this least expensive, most open of sports. So far, we have been the only marathon to have complete live network television coverage. But that is about to change. Boston will follow soon, and Chicago and others. Television decision-makers read the numbers: Our ratings often have surpassed U.S.F.L. football, world-championship tennis, and—with the exception of the World Series—baseball. Our recognition factor matches the Indianapolis 500 auto race or the Kentucky Derby. When television expands coverage to other marathons, the real masses of runners will be reached by the sport, and they will join it.

Much of what we have had to wrestle with in recent years will soon be passé. The questions about prize money should be academic. The hypocrisy and charade have been exposed and are being altered. The ancient Olympics were not amateur games. Amateurism was a more recent idea promulgated by the elitism of upper classes who wanted their sports pure not so much from the taint of money as from the taint of participation by the lower classes. Poor people couldn't afford to join the games; the rich had them to themselves.

The 1984 Olympics reflected the alterations. Many of the athletes were actually professionals earning six-figure incomes in "cleansed" money—prize money laundered through the process of "trust funds." That was just the first step in the right direction. The unrest and disruption of the recent Olympic games can be traced in large measure to persistent hypocrisies—political and financial. But it is the hypocrisies that will die, not the Olympics. I predict that by 1988, more of the taboos will be lifted. Ultimately—perhaps even by 1992—all the hypocrisy of amateurism will be gone. Professionals will be accepted openly, and the games will be for the very best athletes in the world.

A couple of years from now, our New York marathon will come to accept 20,000 runners. My ultimate vision is to have a maximum of 30,000 entrants, using both the upper and lower levels of the Verrazano Bridge as a starting point. It would the most magnificent spectacle of amassed athletes in the history of the world.

By the year 2,000, I predict that men will break the two-hour barrier for the marathon; women will be running at what is now the men's world-record times. (An improvement of just one or two seconds per mile per year will accomplish that.)

By the year 2,000, I will not be president of the New York Road Runners Club or director of the New York City Marathon. But I will still be running. If fate is with me, I will be running in our own marathon right here in New York.

$\int$

Index

The New York Road Runners Club Board of Directors is not just a rubber-stamp board; its members are dedicated runners who care deeply about every aspect of their sport. This is demonstrated most vividly by the impressive number of marathons they personally have participated in. Collectively, they have run 832 marathons to date, and individually their tallies read:

Vincent Chiappetta, 113
Ted Corbitt, 198
Andrew Kimmerling, 7
Joe Kleinerman, 35
Nina Kuscsik, 81
Carl Landegger, 8
Fred Lebow, 58
Arno Neimand, 5
Elizabeth Phillios, 13
Peter Roth, 2
Also Scandurra, 200
Kurt Steiner, 99
Allan Steinfeld, 1
Richard Traum, 5
Stephen Wald, 7